The Sugarcraft Library

Country Flowers

JANE SHARP

Angus&Robertson

An imprint of HarperCollins*Publishers*

Dedication

To John and Elizabeth
for all your love and support

AN ANGUS & ROBERTSON BOOK
An Imprint of HarperCollins Publishers

First published in Australia in 1992 by
Collins, Angus & Robertson Publishers Pty
Limited (ACN 009 913 517)
25–31 Ryde Road, Pymble NSW 2073, Australia

National Library of Australia
Cataloguing-in-Publication data:

Sharp, Jane.
Country Flowers.
Includes index.

ISBN 0 207 17705 8.

1. Cake decorating.   2. Artificial flowers.
3. Sugar art.   I. Title. (Series: Sugarcraft library).

641.8653

Printed in Italy

5 4 3 2 1   92 93 94 95

With many thanks to The Harry Smith Horticultural
Photographic Collection for the photographs of the flowers
which appear on pages 30, 42, 54, 66, 78, 90 and 102.

Contents

Foreword

I have known Jane for several years and have always admired her originality and style. Her flower work is wonderfully detailed, reproducing the exact intricacies, colouring and size of each flower. The instructions for making the flowers are very clear and precise, so even if you do not have access to the real flower you will have no problem in producing the sugar version. In describing the flowers, this book also takes us on a nature trek to many wonderful and varied environments, from the woodland to the seashore and on and up into the mountains.

Jane's inventive cake designs and countryside scenes are all based around the country flowers described in the book, but also use tiny creatures, such as ladybirds, fish and birds, and rocks, logs, pools or stone walls – all made from sugar – to add realism and atmosphere. I hope that you will enjoy looking through this book, as I did, and find pleasure in making the beautiful flowers shown.

NICHOLAS LODGE

Introduction

Wild flowers have been a great love of mine since childhood, and the studying, drawing and painting of all natural objects has been a lifelong pleasure. This background and the more formal skills I acquired at art school inspired me in my present work with sugar – making intricate replicas of country flowers. The results can be wonderfully lifelike and rewarding. Indeed, my copies have even been mistaken for real flowers on occasion, which shows that flower paste is an excellent modelling medium. Sometimes, the minute detail of a petal or leaf defies the sugar medium and compromises have to be made giving the artistic effect if viewed from a slight distance. I recommend that you work from a real flower specimen, whenever possible. There are many wild flowers that can be picked freely as long as the plants themselves are not uprooted.

However, some flowers are rare and protected, so do check with national or local conservation groups first (such as the Department of the Environment in the UK).

If you already make wired flowers and would like to increase your range of skills, I hope this book will provide the guidance you need. As you work through the pages, you will see how the basic techniques can be extended and adapted. For example, I have designed seven cakes which show how the flowers can be used to create stunning cake decorations for all occasions. In each case the flower sprays can be removed and kept as a lasting memento. The flowers can also be used to create the complex countryside scenes also shown here. I hope my ideas and enthusiasm for country flowers will inspire you in your own sugarcraft creations.

JANE SHARP

Equipment

All the flowers and leaves shown in the book can be made from the templates which are provided at the end of each chapter. However, many can also be cut out using special cutters and these are shown in the flower projects. A non-stick rolling board is a great asset to the flower modeller. Choose a coloured one for preference, as it allows you to see the thickness of the paste and it is also better for the eyes when working with white paste.

There are several essential tools you will need to make the flowers and they are pictured on this page. Some of the materials detailed on page 7, such as polystyrene dome (apple) formers, maize (corn) husk, cotton thread and cocktail sticks (toothpicks) are easily obtained. Other items can be purchased from specialist stores (see Suppliers).

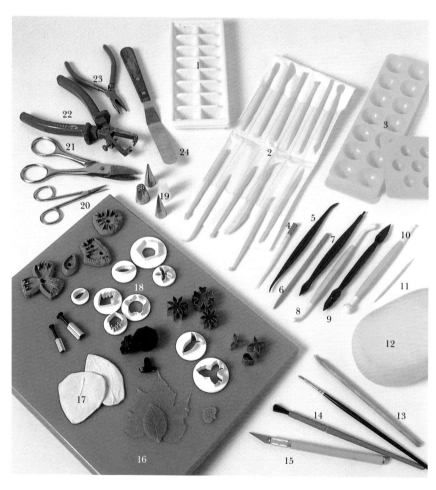

1 *ice-cube palette*
2 *miniature tools (the ball tools are especially useful)*
3 *half-ball moulds for shaping flowers*
4 *porcupine quill or plastic cocktail stick (toothpick) for veining*
5 *grooving tool for insertion-method leaves and petals (see Basic Techniques)*
6 *veining tool*
7 *hollowing tool for opening trumpet flowers*
8 *dog bone tool*
9 *5-pointed star tool*
10 *ball tool*
11 *cocktail sticks (toothpicks)*
12 *baby sponge*
13 *miniature dowel rolling pin*
14 *cheap brushes for dusting and fine sable brush for painting*
15 *modelling knife with an acute-angled blade*
16 *non-stick rolling board*
17 *veiners, purchased and homemade*
18 *cutters*
19 *icing nozzles No. 00, 0, 1, 2, 3 and 'grass'*
20 *small scissors*
21 *florists' wire cutters*
22 *wire strippers*
23 *needle-nose pliers*
24 *angled palette knife (spatula)*

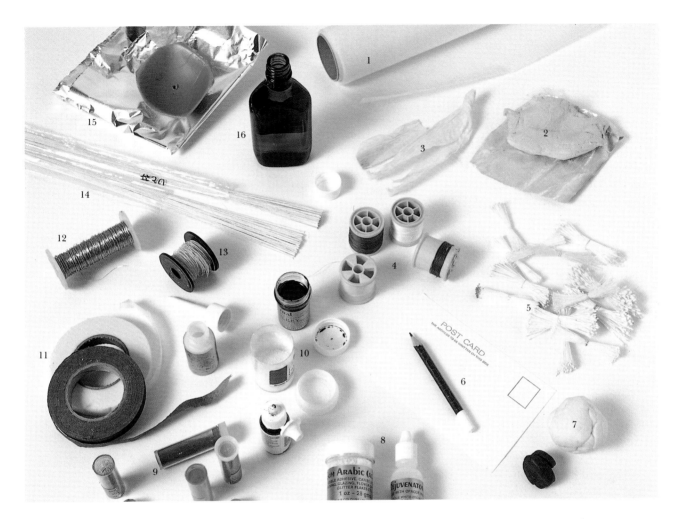

1. *paper towels – use under dusting palettes to prevent too much mess and to remove excess moisture from brushes when painting*
2. *self-hardening modelling clay for making veiners*
3. *maize (corn) husk for veining*
4. *mercerized cotton thread for securing stamens to wire and making stamens*
5. *a selection of stamens*
6. *card and pencil for making templates*
7. *white flower paste and pre-coloured flower paste (see Recipes)*
8. *brilliant white and rejuvenator spirit (mixed together to make an opaque white for painting on sugar)*
9. *dusting colours for flowers and leaves – water is added to paint details*
10. *paste colour for colouring sugar and flower pastes*
11. *stem tape – a paper tape used for binding wires and forming stems (use white for normal use and brown for woody stems)*
12. *binding wire for binding stems and sprays together*
13. *scientific wire – very fine and used for some very small flowers and leaves*
14. *paper-covered wire – made in various thicknesses for mounting the flowers and leaves: 24 gauge for heavier flowers and 26, 28, 30, and 33 gauge for the lighter ones*
15. *polystyrene dome (apple) former – available from greengrocers and used with foil for shaping the winter aconite*
16. *triple-strength rose water – added to gum arabic powder to make a glaze or glue (see Recipes)*

Basic Recipes

FLOWER PASTE

I like my paste to be fairly stiff so that work does not 'wilt'; for a softer paste, add more white vegetable fat. For this recipe only, use *rounded* medicine spoon (teaspoon) measures. This flower paste recipe originates from Denise Fryer of South Africa.

- 450 g (1 lb/4 cups) icing (confectioners') sugar, sifted
- 15 ml (3 tsp) gum tragacanth (the whiter the better)
- 25 ml (5 tsp) cold water
- 10 ml (2 tsp) gelatine
- 10 ml (2 tsp) liquid glucose
- 10 ml (2 tsp) white vegetable fat
- 1 egg white (size 2)

Place the sifted icing sugar and the gum tragacanth into the bowl of a heavy-duty mixer. Cover with a clean cloth and a plate and stand in a pan of simmering water. Heat the beater attachment in the water at the same time.

Put the water in a heatproof glass bowl and sprinkle the gelatine over it. Let it stand until the gelatine mixture becomes spongy, about 5 minutes.

Bring some water to the boil and stand the glucose, still in its jar, in the water to soften. Remove.

Place the gelatine bowl over the hot (not boiling) water until dissolved and clear. Do not allow it to cool or it will start to set. Add the liquid glucose and white vegetable fat to the dissolved gelatine and heat slowly until all the ingredients are combined.

Insert the beater into the mixer. Attach the mixer bowl with the heated sugar and add the dissolved gelatine mixture and the egg white. Cover the bowl with a cloth, initially, and beat at the lowest speed setting for 10 minutes. The paste should become white and stringy. Do not knead the paste, simply seal in a plastic bag, place this in an airtight container and leave in the refrigerator for at least 24 hours.

Tips

Don't leave the room while the machine is operating.
Do use rounded teaspoons – level will make a soft paste and heaped a very hard paste.
Do use paste colour not liquid or powder colour if you wish to colour the paste.

Using the Paste

I prefer the paste to be well matured; after two or three weeks it will be lovely to handle and it can be kept for up to three months. Store in the refrigerator but bring the paste to room temperature before using. The paste will set into a hard lump, but when needed simply break off a small amount and knead a little fat into it to make it more pliable. If the paste should feel too dry, dip it in egg white, dust your hands with icing sugar and knead.

Ready-made pastes can be purchased, but I generally find they are too soft.

PASTILLAGE GUM PASTE

This is a harder and faster-drying paste used mainly for modelling prop items. It must always be stored in an airtight container and will keep for up to three months in the refrigerator. Before using, bring back to room temperature and knead. It can be coloured with paste colour.

- 7.5 ml (1½ tsp) gelatine
- 50 ml (5 dessertsp) cold water
- 450 g (1 lb/4 cups) icing (confectioners') sugar
- 2.5 ml (½ tsp) gum tragacanth
- knob of vegetable fat

Soak the gelatine in the water for one hour.

Warm a bowl containing the icing sugar and the gum tragacanth. This is important to achieve the correct consistency; if the icing is cold the paste will set in spots.

Dissolve the gelatine over hot (not boiling) water, then pour into the warmed sugar stirring with a warm utensil.

Add a knob of vegetable fat and knead until the fat is incorporated and you have a smooth stiff paste. Place in a plastic bag inside an airtight container and leave in the refrigerator for at least 24 hours to mature.

GLUES AND GLAZES

Egg white is a good 'glue' for attaching separate pieces of flower paste together when assembling the flower described in this book. However, gum arabic solution can be used as an alternative; it can also be used to glaze petals and leaves (see Basic Techniques, page 10). Mix as follows:

- *1 part gum arabic powder*
- *3 parts triple-strength rose water*

Dissolve the gum arabic in the rose water in a sterilized heatproof bowl over hot water. When the solution is completely clear, strain into a sterilized screw-top jar.

For a thinner solution use 4 parts rose water to 1 part gum arabic powder.

ROYAL ICING 1

This recipe is for covering and general use.

- *7 g (¼ oz) egg-white substitute powder*
- *60 ml (2 fl oz/4 tbsp) water*
- *450 g (1 lb/4 cups) icing (confectioners') sugar, sifted*
- *2 pinches cream of tartar (tartaric acid)*
- *5 ml (1 tsp) glycerine (optional)*

Dissolve the egg-white substitute powder in the water for 15 minutes. Sieve into a mixer bowl, then mix in the sifted icing sugar and cream of tartar a little at a time by hand until incorporated.

Turn the mixer on and beat at the lowest speed for 5 minutes. Add a teaspoon of glycerine for a softer cut if using the icing to cover a cake.

Store in a glass bowl, covering the surface of the icing with a double layer of clingfilm (plastic wrap). Cover the bowl with another layer of clingfilm, place in an airtight container and store in the refrigerator. It can be kept for about one week.

ROYAL ICING 2

Use this version for fine piped work.

- *1 egg white*
- *225 g (8 oz/2 cups) icing (confectioners') sugar, sifted*
- *pinch cream of tartar (tartaric acid)*

Beat all the ingredients together by hand for 15 minutes. Do not add glycerine.

Store as above.

To 'Let-Down' Royal Icing

For run-out work and for icing boards, royal icing with a softer consistency will be needed. If using the recipe for Royal Icing 1, let-down with water; for Royal Icing 2, let-down with albumen and egg white. Add the liquid gradually, stir and count 10 seconds. At this point, the icing should just run back to smooth. If using to cover a board, leave the icing covered with a damp cloth overnight and stir it gently before use to disperse any air bubbles.

Rolled Fondant (Sugarpaste)

Use ready-made rolled fondant (sugarpaste), available from sugarcraft suppliers, to cover the cakes.

Basic Techniques

As a general rule use white paste, wires and tape and apply dust and liquid colour when the paste is dry to achieve a more natural effect. Colour varies from bud to grown flower and these tones can be adjusted by adding more or less dust. Natural stems are not the basic colour of green wire; they vary from the light green of the growing tip to the reds, browns and purples found at the base. For more information on creating colour effects, see the section on Dust Colouring, page 13. Also, use half-length wires for the flowers so that they are long enough to form 'feet' when making a standing plant. Only use shorter wires if the flower or leaf is to be joined to a longer stem.

MAKING FLOWERS AND LEAVES

The following techniques are used extensively throughout the book. Before attempting a finished flower, practise these methods until you have mastered the steps.

Securing Stamens to Wire

Wild flowers are usually rather small and often there is no calyx to cover the bump formed by a wire attachment. Tape is not strong enough; it can fall

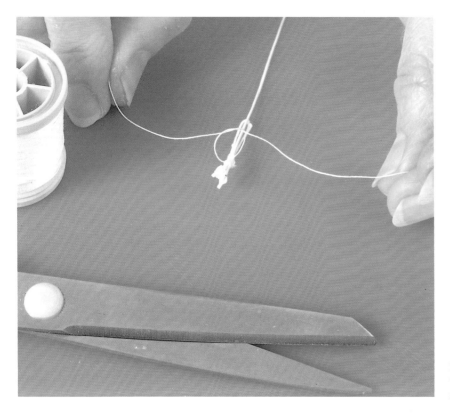

1 Allow several cm (inches) of thread to make tying easier. Knot 2 or 3 times, trim the threads and then trim the base cottons of the stamens at an angle; tape with ⅓-width tape.

apart when the stamens are pushed into the flower. Use mercerized cotton to secure stamens to the base wire; it is fine, nearly invisible and will make a good tight ligature.

Pedestal (Mexican Hat) Method

This technique is used to form many of the flowerheads described in this book.

1 Mould a teardrop or carrot shape (this depends on the thickness and size of the base of the flower). Place the fat end on a board. Using a thin piece of dowel (miniature rolling pin) press down and roll outwards, thinning the base. Lift and turn so that the base is evenly thinned .

2 Place the cutter or template over the pedestal and cut out, then remove the excess paste and push out the shape gently. If using a template, cut a hole in the centre so that it will fit over the pedestal.

Insertion Method

This technique is used for most of the leaves and also some individual petals.

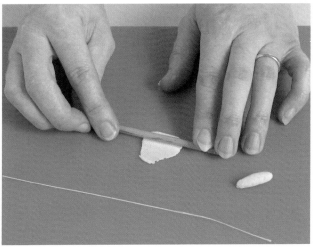

1 Remove 3 mm (1/8″) of paper from a 28 gauge wire with wire strippers. Mould a pea-sized ball of paste into a cigar shape. With a small dowel rolling pin, press down in the centre lengthwise and roll towards the edge.

2 Now press down again in the centre, leaving a narrow ridge, and roll to the opposite edge.

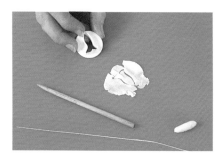

3 Place the dowel across the middle of the ridge at right angles to it and roll outwards, leaving a 1.5 cm (½″) ridge. Thin all round the ridge.

4 Position the leaf or petal cutter or template with the base over the ridge so that approximately 5 mm (¼″) of the ridge remains within the cutter. Cut out and remove the excess.

6 Place on a veiner or the back of a leaf and press firmly; do not touch the ridge.

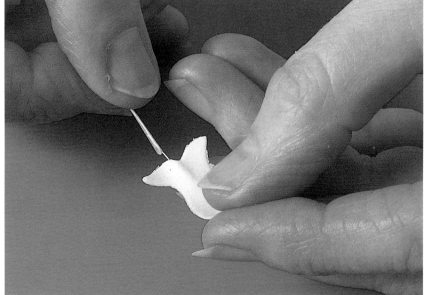

7 Insert the wire, reverse the leaf and crease lengthwise to form a central vein.

5 Place the leaf on the palm and thin the edges with a dog bone tool.

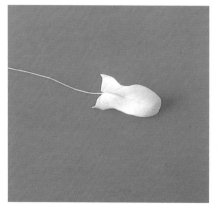

8 Smooth the insertion area on the upper side of the leaf with a fine grooving tool or a cocktail stick. Allow for a longer ridge if the leaf is lobed.

Using Cutters

Roll the flower paste very thin, then slide a palette knife (spatula) under the paste to release it from the board. Position the cutter, press firmly, then remove the excess paste around it. Now remove the cutter and gently push out the shape. Trim with a sharp knife if necessary.

Making Templates

If the right shape or size of cutter is not available, it may be necessary to use templates. Use postcard card and a sharp, fairly hard pencil. Draw carefully around the leaf or flower and cut the template out with small sharp scissors. Make a hole in the centre if it is to be used for a pedestal-method flower.

Enlarging: Draw around the subject, then draw around the outline shape again keeping a uniform distance and echoing the shape.

Reducing: Draw around the subject, then draw again as before but keeping to the inside of the original outline.

DUST COLOURING

Always allow the flower paste to dry before applying dusting colour and keep your colouring and flower-making areas quite separate. An ice-cube tray makes a useful colouring palette because the compartments are deep. Paper towels keep the work surface clean. Use inexpensive paintbrushes for dusting; they must be absolutely dry.

Mixing Colours

Colours straight from the pot are seldom the exact shade you need. Select the basic colour and then gradually add other colours until you have a good match; hold the flowerhead, or whatever, next to the palette and watch the colours match. As with all things, better results come with practice.

All the colours referred to in this book are 'Blossom Tint' by Sugarflair. Other dusting colours can be used, but do practise mixing the colours before embarking on any final colouring as basic shades do vary. For example, 'violet' can be either blue- or pink-based and will produce a different effect.

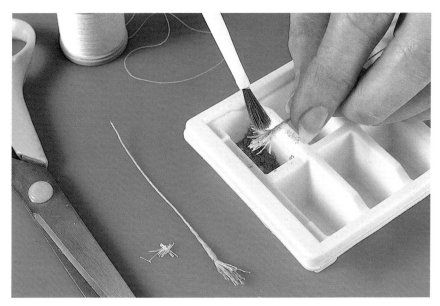

Applying Colour

1 Hold the flower over the palette. Brush with the dust, then tap the stem just below the flower so that excess dust drops back into the palette (no waste or mess).

O v e r - D u s t i n g

Over-dusting with a second colour will produce a very realistic, three-dimensional effect. This technique is often used when colouring leaves.

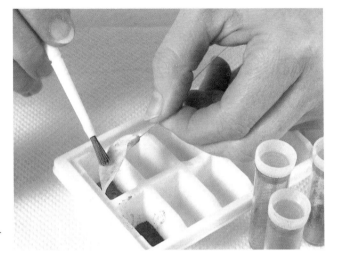

1 Dust the whole leaf the shade of the under side; this is always paler as it does not get as much light.

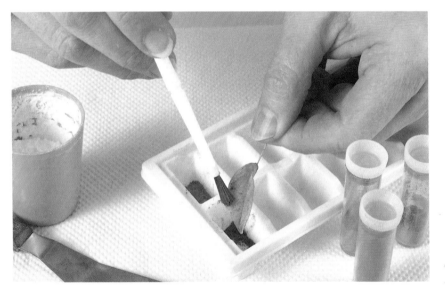

2 Now over-dust the upper surface of the leaf with a deeper shade.

Using Black and White Dusting Colours

A very light dusting of black on the edges of flowers and leaves will create a much more three-dimensional effect. A slight dusting on the calyx will give a shadow effect. A random dusting of white over petals and upper leaves will create a 'bloom'.

Dusting Stems

Once the flowers and leaves have been coloured, steamed and, where applicable, glazed, assemble them into stems using one-third- or half-width white tape. The final step is to colour the stems. Always hold the stem so that the dust falls away from the flowers.

LEAF DETAILS

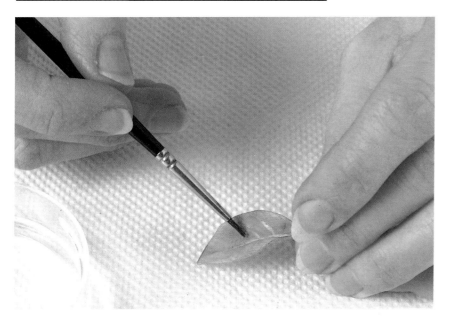

Leaf-Vein Painting

1 Use a fine sable brush and clean water to paint the central vein, removing the top layer of colour to reveal the lighter shade underneath. Work along the lateral veins from the centre petering the lines out to nothing at the leaf edges. Some leaves have individual markings; study and reproduce them by painting with dusting colour and added water.

Veining Moulds

1 Natural leaves can be used to vein sugar replicas but for those times of the year when they are not available it is useful to have ready a selection of leaf moulds made from self-hardening clay. Roll out a portion of clay, larger than the leaf itself, on a piece of wax paper. Place the back of the leaf on the clay and gently roll with a rolling pin. Carefully remove the leaf. Remove the paper when the clay is dry enough to handle. Turn the clay mould over frequently so it dries flat. This is the negative. To make the positive mould, roll out another piece of clay and press the negative mould into it (as illustrated). This will resemble the back of the leaf.

Furry Effect on Leaves

1 Edelweiss and pasqueflower, for example, have naturally downy leaves. Assemble and arrange the plants, then lightly paint over the surfaces to be furred with a clean, moist sable brush and sprinkle with castor (superfine) sugar.

STEAMING

Once all the colouring is complete, the flower pieces will be ready for steaming. This achieves several things: it consolidates the dusting colours so specks of powder do not fall on to the cake; it melts a layer of the sugar making the flowers thinner and more translucent; it strengthens the flower paste and adds a slight sheen.

Use a small kettle that does not automatically switch off at boiling point. Fill to 2.5 to 5 cm (1 to 2″). Have all the flowers and leaves by the kettle and some polystyrene and straight-sided jars ready to receive the treated pieces. All pieces must be fully coloured and quite dry before steaming. Holding by the end of the wire, bring each piece through the steam as near as possible to the spout and place to dry. Put large or heavy pieces in individual jars, and arrange smaller pieces on polystyrene. Do not handle or allow the pieces to touch each other and do not hold them in the steam for too long, or they will melt.

GLAZING

Some flower petals and leaves (for example, the celandine) need a shinier finish than is achieved by just steaming. Gently paint the dry petals and leaves with gum arabic (see Basic Recipes, page 8) or ready-made confectioners' glaze. Dry overnight as described for steaming.

Finishing Techniques

The flowers in this book can be used as simple spray decorations. However, if you wish to make 'standing' flower groups, or would like to create some of the scenes described for the cakes and tableaux, the following techniques will show how to achieve a professional finish.

BASES

Look out for interesting surfaces and shapes to use as bases – cork, wood, marble, glass and basketwork are typical examples. Attach a small thin cakeboard to your selected base. Secure by drilling small holes through both the board and base and tie with flower wire so that the joins appear on the top surface. Cover with rolled fondant (sugarpaste), then texture and paint using liquid colour. **Do not put any wires into a cake.**

Covering Boards with Icing

Use let-down royal icing (see Basic Recipes, page 8). Apply the icing to the board edge with a small palette knife; smooth and wipe the board edge with a damp cloth. Set to dry under two 60-watt lamps positioned 30 cm (12″) above the board and leave for about an hour, turning the cake every 10 minutes. Alternatively, cover the board with rolled fondant (sugarpaste) before covering the cake.

A selection of cork, basketwork and wooden bases.

17

LIGHT SOURCE AND SHADOW

When creating a three-dimensional natural scene remember that the 'sun' is shining from a particular direction – from directly above or maybe slanting in from either the left or right side. This means that all surfaces facing that direction would be illuminated and should therefore appear lighter and areas facing away from the light source would be in shadow. On rocks, ground, logs, or whatever, paint the areas in 'shadow' with deeper shades of colour, *but not black*. By deepening the background colour, the flowers and foliage will be brought more to the fore, creating a three-dimensional scene.

WIRE SUPPORTS FOR STANDING PLANTS

This technique is used for assembled flowers which need to stand upright. Make the stems of the individual flowers following the instructions.

SCENE PROPS

Effective scene props can be modelled with rolled fondant (sugarpaste) or pastillage and then coloured.

Rocks: Mould with 'short', drying pastillage and left-over flower paste. When dry, place on paper towels and brush with liquid colour, rolling the mould over with the brush as you go.

Boulders and pebbles: Mould with rolled fondant (sugarpaste). When dry, paint with liquid colour on paper towels.

Sand: Sprinkle the chosen base with semolina, adding some cream dusting colour for a deeper shade. Soft brown sugar also gives a realistic effect.

Snow: Cover the selected surface with rough royal icing. Allow to dry, then paint the snow surface with a clean moist brush and sprinkle with castor (superfine) sugar.

Logs: Mould from drying white pastillage then crisscross with a cocktail stick (toothpick) or porcupine quill to imitate bark. Paint, when dry, with liquid colours.

1 Assemble the component parts of the plant in the hand and tie the stems together with binding wire just below the 'ground' level. Position the plant on the selected base, then divide the stem wires and bend them at right angles to form three 'feet'. Trim the bent wires to approximately 2.5–4 cm (1–1½"). The plant will now stand unsupported. The plants can then be moved around to obtain the best balance of design. Secure with royal icing and cover the 'feet' with undergrowth, stones or other suitable props.

Various modelled and painted scene props.

cut strips to the required height and fringe with a modelling knife. Paint the base with egg white and roll up. Place in position with curved tweezers.

Dry-stone wall: Mould various sizes of stones with pastillage or rolled fondant (sugarpaste) that is beginning to dry and lightly paint with greys, blues and greens. Assemble with as little royal icing as possible and support while drying. Finish the top with a row of stones standing on end. When dry, pipe on moss and lichen; this will strengthen the structure, as well as making the wall look suitably weathered.

A detail showing a dry-stone wall and piped grass.

Moss: Use white royal icing and a fine No.00 or 0 nozzle to pipe squiggles on to the log or stones. Dry and paint yellow/green. Remember, moss grows on the north-facing sides of objects.

Water effects: Paint lightly coloured green-blue piping jelly over stones to make a stream, creating an uneven surface for ripples. For a flat pond, thin with alcohol and warm slightly to run into a depression.

Muddy puddles: Smear mud-coloured royal icing on to the surface with a small palette knife (spatula) and paint in the puddle with piping jelly. Mix the royal icing and piping jelly at the edges of the puddle with a brush.

Dead leaves: Cut out flat oak or beech leaves from flower paste, curl and crumple and, when dry, dust with skin tone and black.

Grass: Use stiff, white royal icing and a grass nozzle. When *completely* dry, paint in shades of blue, green, yellow and brown. Alternatively, using flower paste,

The talking point: To add a little something extra, choose a fish, bird, butterfly, beetle or hedgehog, for example, to complete your nature scene. Use a nature book for reference, draw and make templates from cardboard and mould in rolled fondant (sugarpaste) or pastillage. Pipe on fur with royal icing; feathers can be cut from flower paste. Paint with liquid colours and dust fish with snowflake dust for a shimmering effect.

Heralds
of Spring

It is very exciting after the long drab winter months to find the first flowers of spring: a carpet of bright yellow winter aconites and dainty white snowdrops, blue Siberian squill and hazel trees with new catkins.

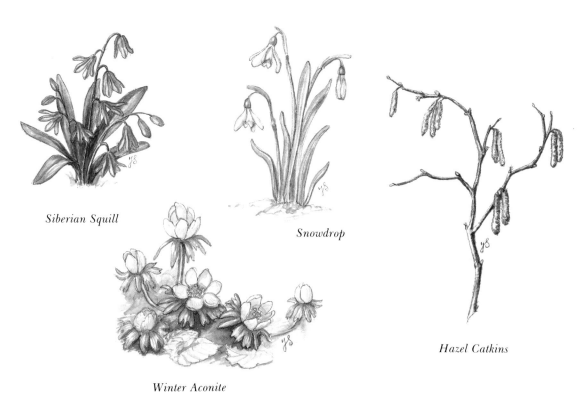

Siberian Squill

Snowdrop

Winter Aconite

Hazel Catkins

Winter Engagement Cake

This double heart-shaped cake has been designed with Valentines in mind. The snowdrop design is piped on to a piece of pliable perspex and then pressed on to the sides of the cake before the rolled fondant (sugarpaste) covering has dried, and the cake then dusted a pale green colour. The leaves are brush embroidered and the snowdrops pressure piped with royal icing, and then coloured. The rings are moulded from flower paste and the snow is formed from royal icing. The flower sprays are positioned, together with the stones and dead leaves, and the snow areas are finally painted with water and sprinkled with castor (superfine) sugar.

THE FLOWER SPRAYS

- *3 snowdrops with 2 buds and 2 small, 3 medium and 1 large leaves*
- *2 winter aconites with 2 buds*
- *3 branches of catkins*
- *2 groups of Siberian squill with 3 flowers, 1 opening flower, 4 buds and 2 small and 2 large leaves*

Winter Aconite

Eranthis hyemalis

The winter aconite, a member of the buttercup family, is one of the earliest spring flowers to appear. The flower has six petals, three larger than the others, and a set of leaves that form a ruff surrounding the flower.

REQUIREMENTS

● *Medium and small cream or white pointed stamens;* ● *24 gauge white wire;* ● *white tape* ● *white cotton thread;* ● *cocktail stick (toothpick);* ● *white flower paste;* ● *small ball tool;* ● *sponge;* ● *porcupine quill;* ● *foil;* ● *dome (apple) former covered with foil;* ● *glue;* ● *paper clips;* ● *maize (corn) husk;* ● *fine sable brush;* ● *royal icing;* ● *small nozzle and piping bag;* ● *cornflour (cornstarch);* ● *dusting colours in moss-green, apple-green, lemon-yellow, egg-yellow, cornflower-blue, skin tone, black, white.*

1 **STAMENS:** Take 6 medium stamen heads and tie to a wire, holding the points tightly together to form a cone; trim the ends. Dust with moss-green colour. Surround just below the central cone with small stamens (30–40 heads). Tie, trim and bind with ⅓-width tape. Curve the heads inwards with a cocktail stick. Dust with lemon.

RUFF: Cut out a ruff from thin paste. Reverse on the palm of the hand and thin the edges with a ball tool. Vein on maize. Lightly roll inside the edges.

2 Turn the ruff over and place on the former, then push the stamen wire through all the thicknesses. Position the stamens so they sit just above the ruff and secure with glue. Fold the wire underneath the former and secure with a paper clip. Crumple the foil to give the ruff an uneven, natural look, support on a cup or jar and allow to dry. For a less open flower, make the ruff as above but dry on a concave former.

3 **PETALS:** Cut out 3 narrow and 3 fatter petals from thinly rolled flower paste. Thin the edges with a small ball tool. Press on to a piece of maize husk to vein. Lightly roll just inside the edge with the ball tool to curve the petal, then place on a sponge and re-mark the veins with a porcupine quill. Dry in a small cupped former. Curl the tips inwards for the less open flowers.

4 **COLOURING AND FLOWER ASSEMBLY:** Dust the petals with lemon and a touch of moss-green, mixed with cornflour to lighten. Dust both sides of the ruff with moss/cornflour; over-dust the upper side with apple-green and a little cornflower-blue and cornflour. Paint in the veins, removing the top layer of dust to reveal the under colour. Place back on the former. Stick the 3 large petals over the gaps in the ruff with a little royal icing and support with small balls of foil. Add the 3 thin petals between and over the first layer, and dry well. Dust the ruff edges with light skin tone and dust the petals again with lemon/egg-yellow/cornflour. Random dust the petals with white and flick dust the petals and the ruff edges with a tiny amount of black. Steam and dry.

5 **ASSEMBLY:** Arrange the flowers in small sprays and display growing out from snow. The bud is made from smaller templates of the petals and ruff, as follows. Make a hook on a 24 gauge wire, cover with a small pea-sized ball of paste and dry. Cut out 3 of each petal shape. Wrap the 3 narrow petals over the central ball and trim at the base. Now wrap the larger petals over the first layer, alternating them. Trim and dry upside down. Colour with lemon with a little moss-green added. Attach a ruff fairly tightly around the bud; colour the inside before positioning.

Snowdrop

Galanthus nivalis

The single flower of the snowdrop opens from a small sheath, like its relative the daffodil. The three outer petals are white while the three inner ones are tipped with a 'horseshoe' of green.

REQUIREMENTS
- *White flower paste;* ● *very small cream or white stamens;* ● *28 and 30 gauge white wire;* ● *white tape;*
- *white cotton thread;* ● *wire-strippers;*
- *fine sable brush;* ● *small ball tool;*
- *glue;* ● *small needle-nose pliers;*
- *maize (corn) husk;* ● *grooving tool;*
- *dog bone tool;* ● *binding wire;*
- *cornflour (cornstarch);* ● *dusting colours in apple-green, moss-green, lemon-yellow, egg-yellow, cornflower-blue, black, white.*

1 STAMENS: Take a half 30 gauge wire and strip 3 cm (1¼″) of the covering from one end. Tie 5 stamen heads to it and bind with narrow stem tape to create a very fine centre and stem. Paint the stamens with egg-yellow mixed with a little water.

INNER PETALS: Cut out 3 small petals and keep covered. Reverse one on the palm with the base towards you and hollow, using a small ball tool. Repeat with the other two. Paint a tiny horseshoe shape on the hollowed side only with apple-green dust mixed with a little water.

2 Moisten the petals with a little glue and attach one petal at a time with a pinch at the base to the stamen wire. Dry upside down. Paint the horseshoe shape on the outside of each petal.

OUTER PETALS: Cut out the 3-petalled shape from thin paste. With a small ball tool stroke the petals towards the outer points. Vein on maize husk. Cup each petal and thread on to the wire; they should alternate with the inner petals. Thread a tiny ball of paste on to the wire, mould into an ovary at the flower base and dry.

3 **SHEATH:** Cut out a small leaf shape. Stroke towards the point to stretch it and vein by sandwiching beteen two layers of maize. Hollow the sheath and apply glue to the base. Curve the stem immediately behind the ovary using small needle-nose pliers and secure the sheath about 1 cm (⅜″) down the stem so that it curves towards the flower.

BUD: Form a hook on a 30 gauge wire. Mould a small ball of paste into a cigar shape. Twist with the first finger and thumb to tighten on to the wire. Add a tiny ball of paste to the base for the ovary. Attach a sheath, positioned closer to the bud than it is on the flower.

4 **LEAVES:** Make in 3 sizes as follows. Remove about 2 cm (¾″) of paper from a 28 gauge wire using wire strippers. Mould a 1 cm (⅜″) diameter ball of paste into a sausage 4 cm (1½″) long. Form a leaf using the insertion method (see Basic Techniques, page 11), making a 3 cm (1¼″) ridge, trimmed to 2.5 cm (1″) once cut out. Place on maize to vein. Fold in half lengthwise to make the central vein and hollow between the ridge and the outer edges. Moisten the stripped wire with glue and insert into the ridge, then reverse on the palm and form a groove into the wired area with a grooving tool. Dry so that the tip of the leaf curves backwards.

5 **COLOURING AND ASSEMBLY:** Paint the ovary and upper stem with moss-green liquid colour with a little lemon and cornflour added. Dust the stem and sheath with powder colour in the same shades. Dust the leaves with moss-green/cornflour-blue with a little cornflour added. Over-dust the upper side of the leaves with a deeper shade of moss/cornflour-blue by adding less cornflour. Random dust the leaves, buds and flowers with white dust and then edge dust with black. Steam.

Hold several flowers and buds in a group. Arrange various sized leaves around them so the bases of the leaves are level. Tie at 'ground' level with binding wire and form a standing 'foot'.

Siberian Squill

Scilla siberica

The scillas are members of the bluebell family but bloom earlier in the year. The flowers have blue, six-pointed petals with a darker central stripe. Three to four bells hang from each stem.

REQUIREMENTS
- *White flower paste;* ● *small pale yellow ball stamens;* ● *white cotton thread;* ● *33 gauge white wire;*
- *fine sable brush;* ● *porcupine quill or plastic cocktail stick (toothpick);* ● *cocktail stick (toothpick);* ● *white stem tape;*
- *glue;* ● *miniature dowel rolling pin;* ● *trumpet hollowing tool;*
- *small scissors;* ● *needle-nose pliers;* ● *maize (corn) husk;* ● *small ball tool;* ● *binding wire;* ● *cornflour (cornstarch);* ● *dusting colours in apple- and moss-green, lemon-yellow, cornflower-blue, black, brown, rose-pink, white.*

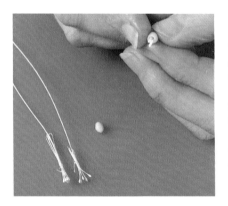

1 STAMENS: Take 6 stamen heads and tie to a half wire. Place the wire 3 mm (⅛″) below the stamens, tie and tape below this position so the stamens are level. For the ovary, mould a very small ball of paste to the stamen wire 3 mm (⅛″) below the base of the stamen heads. Splay out the heads, colour the ball moss/lemon and dry. Paint the stamen heads with cornflower-blue/black with a little water added.

2 FLOWER: Using the pedestal method (see Basic Techniques, page 11), cut out a 6-pointed flower. Hold the pointed base in the left hand and push the trumpet hollowing tool into the centre to hollow. Hollow and stroke towards the point of each petal with a small ball tool. Place the point of the porcupine quill into the flower centre and draw out along the centre of each petal to form a groove. Cut in between the petals with scissors to remove a small triangle about 3 mm (⅛″) deep.

3 Thread the stamen wire through the flower and attach with a little glue below the ovary. Form the base of the flower into a bulbous shape by rolling between the fingers. Kink the petals with a cocktail stick. Tweak the petals into slightly different positions.

4 **LEAF:** Make using the snowdrop insertion method (see page 24).
OPENING FLOWER: Make as for the flower but do not cut between the petals; mould to a hooked wire. Lightly touch the inside of the petals with glue so they hold together.
BUD: Mould a bud to a wire and taper. Make in 3 sizes from 5 mm–1 cm (¼–⅜″) long – the larger sizes should be more bulbous.
COLOURING THE FLOWER: Mix cornflower-blue/cornflour and a touch of rose-pink. Dust inside and out leaving the base of the flower very pale. Mix a slightly darker blue with water and paint fine lines down the centre of each petal inside and outside. Allow to dry. Random dust with rose/cornflower-blue. Colour the opening flowers and buds in the same way.

5 **COLOURING THE LEAVES:** Dust the upper and lower sides with moss/cornflour. Over-dust the upper side with apple-green/brown and a little cornflour. Edge dust leaves and flowers with black. Blush with white. Steam and dry well.
ASSEMBLY: Curve the wires next to the flower with needle-nose pliers. Take a small bud, tape a larger bud to it 1 cm (⅜″) down. Add an opening bud and a flower. Make up several stems. Dust the stems with moss-green and over-dust the upper stem with rose/blue. Bend the stems with flowers to one side. To assemble a standing plant, hold 3 or 4 stems at 'ground' level and arrange four leaves around with the wires below 'ground' level. Tie below the leaves with binding wire, trim the wires to about 5 cm (2″) and bend to form three horizontal 'feet'.

Hazel Catkins
Corylus avellana

The hazel or cobnut is a common shrub that was often coppiced, the wood being used to make sheep hurdles and wattle for buildings. Early in the season, the yellow male catkins or 'lamb's tails' hang from bare branches where the tiny red female flowers are also to be found. The leaves appear after flowering.

REQUIREMENTS

● *Medium, round-headed, pale yellow stamens;* ● *33 and 24 gauge white wire;* ● *wire strippers;* ● *small needle-nose pliers;* ● *white flower paste;* ● *castor (superfine) sugar;* ● *egg white;* ● *brown stem tape;* ● *demerara (light brown) sugar;* ● *fine sewing needle;* ● *white cotton thread;* ● *gum arabic solution;* ● *cornflour (corn-starch);* ● *dusting colours in moss-green, lemon-yellow, cream, brown.*

1 CATKINS: These can be attached to wire or cotton thread. For wired catkins, cut a 33 gauge wire in three and remove 2 cm (¾") of paper from one end with the strippers. Mould a small piece of paste in a thin sausage approximately 2.5 cm (1") long and thread the wire into one end. Mould to the wire and shape; the base of the catkin should be thinner than the top.

Alternatively, thread a long length of thread on to a fine sewing needle. Mould a small ball of paste into a thin sausage approximately 2.5 cm (1") long. Push the needle through the full length of the sausage leaving 7.5 cm (3") of the thread protruding at one end. Trim the thread at the other end close to the paste and dry. Make several others, varying the size.

2 **COLOURING:** Submerge the whole catkin in egg white and drain. Now dip in a mixture of castor sugar and cream dusting colour, with a touch of moss-green added. Completely coat with the sugar mixture. Curve the wire adjoining the catkin with pliers, shape the catkin into a vague 'S' curve and dry.

For the more open catkins, dip in demerara sugar with a little moss-green dusting colour added.

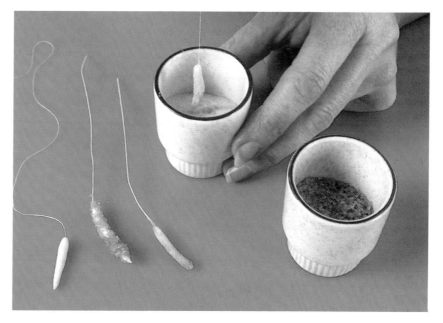

3 **ASSEMBLY:** Tape 1 round-headed stamen just above the end of a half 24 gauge wire with ⅓-width brown tape. The stamen represents the leaf bud. Tape down 1 cm (⅜″) and add a small catkin and a bud just above it. Continue in this way spacing the catkins further apart and adding them in groups of 2 or 3. Make several branches of 2 to 3 groups. These can be used as single branches or they can be taped together to form a tree. Add short bare twigs for more realism and bend into a natural shape with pliers.

Finally, dust the buds with lemon/cornflour with a little moss-green added. Random dust the catkins with brown and then green/yellow. Dust the stems with brown to darken, then glaze with gum arabic solution.

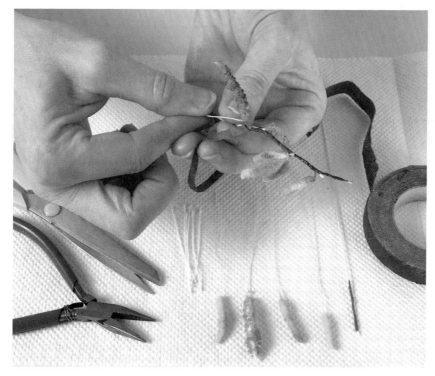

WINTER ACONITE

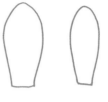

large/small petals

ruff

SNOWDROP

outer petals   *inner petal*   *sheath*

leaves

SIBERIAN SQUILL

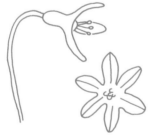

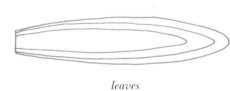

leaves

flower

HAZEL CATKINS

Churchyard Flowers Scene

KEY TO THE DIAGRAM:
1 *basketwork dish*
2 *10 stones in pastillage*
3 *snow made in royal icing and castor (superfine) sugar*
4 *15 dead oak leaves*
5 *3 stems of ivy*
6 *bluetit*
7 *3 branches of hazel with 11 catkins*
8 *snowdrops with 5 flowers, 2 buds, and 8 small, 3 medium and 3 large leaves*
9 *Siberian squill with 10 flowers, 4 buds, and 4 small and 4 large leaves*
10 *winter aconites with 3 flowers and 1 bud.*

Composition

An upturned basketwork dish forms the base of this arrangement. It is supported underneath with a cake drum and above with a thin cakeboard, which is covered with textured rolled fondant (sugarpaste).

A tree of catkins, placed at the back of the scene with large stones at its base, is entwined with ivy. Two more stems of ivy creep over the stones. The snowdrops are growing in two groups on the left-hand side with the bluetit in front of them. The bird is made from pastillage with a flower paste tail and wing feathers; it is supported on wire legs. The scillas are also in two groups, with the winter aconites growing out of the snow.

The snow was roughly spread on with a palette knife (spatula) and the leaves were then scattered with small stones. When it was quite dry the icing was painted with a moist brush and sprinkled with castor (superfine) sugar to imitate snow falling.

Woodland Flowers

In early spring, the woodland floor bursts into life before the trees open their leaves. The blackthorn, or sloe, has clouds of white blossoms that contrast with the stark, spiky branches. Dainty wood anemones flutter to form an ever changing carpet in the wind, shy violets peep through the undergrowth and the bold lesser celandine opens its petals to the sun.

Wood Anemone

Lesser Celandine

Sweet Violet

Blackthorn

Easter Cake

The cake is covered with pale blue rolled fondant (sugarpaste) to represent the sky, and the cakeboard is flooded with let-down royal icing and coloured light tan to form the base of the woodland floor. A curve is cut from the cake to make an alcove for the flower sprays. The background grass is painted on, as are the clouds, in brilliant white. More grass is piped on with stiff royal icing. The stones and dead leaves are positioned and then the flower sprays are stuck in place, held firm with more piped grass and moulded stones.

THE FLOWER SPRAYS

- 9 blackthorn blossoms, 6 opening buds, 18 buds
- 2 wood anemones, with 1 opening bud, 2 buds and 6 groups of 3 leaves
- 3 celandines, with 2 opening buds and 4 small, 4 medium and 2 large leaves
- 3 violets, with 1 opening bud, 1 bud and 2 small, 3 medium and 2 large leaves

Wood Anemone

Anemone nemorosa

Wood anemones are common springtime flowers, usually found in deciduous woods. They have white flowers of six or more petals, often tinged on the back with pink. Three sets of leaves grow below each flower.

REQUIREMENTS

● *White flower paste;* ● *26 and 33 gauge white wire;* ● *tiny, pale yellow seedhead stamens;* ● *white tape;* ● *white cotton thread;* ● *maize (corn) husk or crêpe paper;* ● *3 mm (¹/₈″) dowel rolling pin;* ● *wire strippers;* ● *small needle-nose pliers;* ● *baby sponge;* ● *small ball tool;* ● *maple-leaf veiner;* ● *binding and scientific wire;* ● *glue;* ● *cornflour (cornstarch);* ● *dusting colours in moss-green, apple-green, red, rose-pink, brown, lemon-yellow, black, white.*

1 **STAMENS:** Take 25 strands of seedhead stamens. Keeping the heads fairly level, fold the strands to make 50 heads. Place a 26 gauge wire 5 mm (¹/₄″) below the heads and tie tightly. Trim and bind with ¹/₃-width tape. Press into the middle of the stamen heads, pushing the stamens evenly outwards. Mould a tiny ball of paste, push it into the centre (impaling it on the end of the wire) and attach with glue. Prick it all over with a pin and dry. Paint the centre with moss-green/lemon mixed with water. Paint the stamens with lemon-yellow mixed with water.

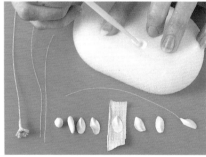

2 **PETALS:** Make 6 petals following the basic instructions for the insertion method (see Basic Techniques, page 11). However, form a 5 mm (¹/₄″) ridge, trim to 3 mm (¹/₈″) once the petal has been cut out and vein on a maize husk or crêpe paper. Pinch the edge on the veined side to form a ridge. Hollow either side of the ridge very lightly. Thread a 10 cm (4″) length of scientific wire into the stem ridge, cup the petal a little on a piece of sponge and allow to dry. The 3 inner petals can curve in a little more than the outer ones.

3 **FLOWER ASSEMBLY:** Bend each petal backwards 30 degrees. Arrange 3 inner petals around the stamens and tie with thread. Now add the other 3 petals between and behind the first layer. Tie securely and tape. There is no calyx. The flower can be all white or light pink on the under side of the petals. Blush the backs of the petals with rose/cornflour. Colour the stems red/brown.

4 **LEAVES:** Using 33 gauge wire and the insertion method (see Basic Techniques, page 11), cut out the larger leaf and ball around the ends. Vein the leaf, then insert the wire and fold along the centre rib. Open out and curve backwards. Cut out a pair of leaves from the smaller cutter and allow to dry.

Colour the leaves with moss-green, adding cornflour to lighten. Over-dust the upper side of the leaf with apple-green/cornflour. Dust the edges with a very little red. Blush with apple-green. Colour the stems green and over-dust with red/brown.

Assemble a leaf stalk by taking a pair of smaller leaves and taping them to a larger leaf. Cover the wires with the tape.

5 **BUDS AND ASSEMBLY:** To make an opening bud, mould a pea-sized ball of paste on to a hooked 26 gauge wire and dry. Cover with 4–5 petals cut from flat paste (do not insert wires).

To make a closed bud, form a pea-sized ball of paste into a rounded fat teardrop. Insert a hooked 26 gauge wire into the pointed end and mould to the wire. Blush the lower part rose and colour the stem brown.

Assemble 3 groups of leaves about 2.5–4 cm (1–1½″) down from the flower, tape and colour brown. Make other groups with buds and opening buds.

Lesser Celandine
Ranunculus ficara

The celandine is a member of the buttercup family but is more daisy-like in appearance with eight to twelve shiny yellow petals which whiten as they age. The flowers are surrounded by a cushion of fleshy, dark green heart-shaped leaves. Celandines are frequently found growing in hedgerows, woods and damp ground.

REQUIREMENTS
● *White flower paste;* ● *medium seedhead yellow stamens;*
● *26 and 28 gauge white wire;*
● *semolina;* ● *yellow cotton thread;* ● *cocktail stick (toothpick);*
● *glue;* ● *2 cm (⅞″) daisy cutter;*
● *small snowdrop cutter;* ● *corn-flour (cornstarch);* ● *porcupine quill or plastic cocktail stick (toothpick);* ● *wire strippers;*
● *dog bone tool;* ● *small ball tool;*
● *small dowel rolling pin;* ● *gum arabic solution;* ● *dusting colours in moss-green, lemon-yellow, cornflower-blue, black, white.*

1 **STAMENS:** Attach a *very* small ball of paste to one end of a half 26 gauge wire. Dip in glue and then in semolina mixed with a little lemon/moss dust and allow to dry. Take 12 strands of stamens, fold in half and bring the 24 heads fairly level. Hold between the finger and thumb so that just 1 cm (⅜″) of the cottons show. Push the stamen heads out evenly and push the wire through the centre bringing the central ball 3 mm (⅛″)

below the heads. Tie with thread, trim and bind with ⅓-width tape. Curl the stamens towards the centre with a cocktail stick. Paint the stamens with lemon mixed with water.

FLOWER: Cut an 8-petalled flower from thin paste and stretch and thin the edges of each petal with a dog bone tool. Vein with a porcupine quill, thread on to the wire and attach behind the stamens with glue. For a more advanced flower, repeat as above but ball just inside the tip of the petals so they roll backwards. Tweak the petals to give a natural look and allow to dry. Colour the flower with lemon mixed with a touch of moss/cornflour.

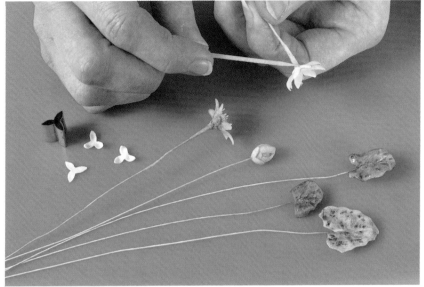

2 **CALYX:** Use a very small snowdrop cutter to cut out the calyx, then reverse on the hand. Hollow the 3 petals with a small ball tool and attach to the base of the flower. Colour the calyx and stem with moss/lemon/cornflour, and over-dust the under side of the flower petals.

BUDS: To make a bud, mould a small teardrop-shaped piece of paste on to a hooked 28 gauge wire. Impress the outline of petals using the cutter. For an opening bud, mould a small pea-sized ball of paste to a 26 gauge wire and allow to dry. Cut out a flower, reverse on the palm, stretch and ball and close over the ball.

3 **LEAVES:** Use the insertion method (see Basic Techniques, page 11). Place the leaf on the palm and thin the edges. Vein on the back of a real leaf or veiner and define the veins with a porcupine quill. Ball the inside edges of the back of the leaf. Insert the wire into the ridge. Squeeze the centre of the leaf and roll back the edges.

To colour, dust both sides and the stem of the leaves with moss-green mixed with a touch of lemon/cornflour. Over-dust the top of the leaf with moss mixed with a touch of yellow/cornflower-blue, but no cornflour. Paint the central vein with clean water, removing the upper layer of dust to reveal the under colour. Work out along the lateral veins to nothing at the leaf edges. Edge dust with black. Random dust with white for a 'bloom'.

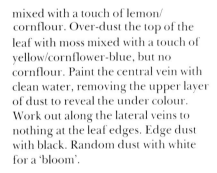

4 **ASSEMBLY:** Steam, then when dry, glaze the upper petals of the flowers and the upper surface of the leaves with gum arabic solution. Tape a pair of small leaves 2.5–4 cm (1–1½") down a flower stem. Make several stems using flowers, opening flowers and buds. Hold as a bunch with the flowers higher than the buds. Add several more buds, then surround with larger leaves. Tie at 'ground' level with binding wire. Splay the wires out to form 'feet' to support the plant.

Sweet Violet
Viola odorata

This lovely sweet-scented flower is surrounded with low-growing heart-shaped leaves. A springtime flower, it is found in woods and hedgerows. The flowers can be blue or red-violet or white. A bunch of violets is a traditional gift on Mothering Sunday.

REQUIREMENTS
- *White flower paste;* ● *medium round-headed white stamens;*
- *26 and 28 gauge white wire;*
- *binding wire;* ● *tape;* ● *needle-nose pliers;* ● *small 5-petal blossom cutter;* ● *small ball tool;* ● *leaf veiner;*
- *baby sponge;* ● *10 cm (4")*
length of 3 mm (⅛") dowel; ● *glue;*
- *gum arabic solution;* ● *cornflour (cornstarch);* ● *dusting colours in tangerine, violet, cornflower-blue, moss-green, apple-green, black, white.*

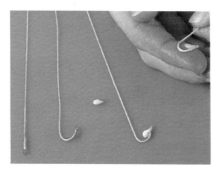

1 STAMENS: Tie 1 stamen head to a 26 gauge wire with thread. Colour with tangerine mixed with water. Bend the wire with pliers. Trim and tape.

SPUR: Mould a tiny ball of paste into a teardrop. Paint the inside of the wire below the stamen with glue and squeeze the pointed end of the teardrop on to the wire. Press the spur flat with the finger and thumb. Dry.

2 LARGE LOWER PETAL: To make the veiner, cut a 10 cm (4") length from a piece of 3 mm (⅛") dowel. Mould a bud-shaped piece of paste to

one end, ridge lengthwise with a knife and dry. Cut 1 large petal from thin paste and thin the edges with a small ball tool. Vein with the dowel veiner inside the edge of the petal. Moisten the base and squeeze with the finger and thumb so that it sticks on to the under side of the spur and dry.

SIDE PETALS: Cut out a pair, place on the palm and thin the edges with a small ball tool. Press the veiner over the whole petal, reverse it and ball inside the top edge so it rolls backwards. Moisten on the veined side and apply to each side of the large petal.

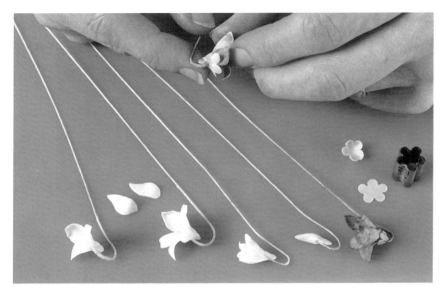

3 **UPPER WINGED PETALS:** Prepare as for the side petals. Moisten the veined side and attach to the upper part of the flower. Roll the petal backwards. Apply the second petal so that it slightly overlaps the first. Dry.

BUDS: Form a small carrot-shaped piece of paste, pinch the fat end to flatten into a spur and insert a 26 gauge wire just below this. Curve the wire with the spur inside it. Curve the bud upwards. For an opening bud, make a bud and dry. Cut out smaller petals and attach to the bud and arrange.

COLOURING THE FLOWER: Dust the flower and buds with violet/cornflower-blue/cornflour. Leave the centre around the stamen white. Random over-dust with cornflower-blue mixed with a little violet. Paint lines on the large lower petal in blue/violet with water added.

CALYX: Cut a small 5-petal blossom, cup on a sponge and thread on to the back of the flower. The spur should poke out between two of the petals.

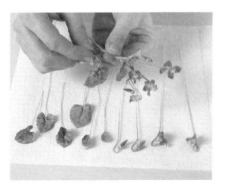

4 **LEAVES:** Make using the insertion method (see Basic Techniques, page 11). Place on the palm and random ball the lobes at the base with a ball tool. Insert the wire into the ridge on the back of the leaf. An opening leaf will unroll and as it grows it will curl back at the point.

Dust the leaves with moss-green mixed with a little cornflower-blue/cornflour. Dust the upper side with moss/apple/cornflower-blue/cornflour.

5 **FINAL COLOURING AND ASSEMBLY:** Dust the calyx and stem with moss-green/cornflour. Over-dust the upper stem with violet/blue. Edge dust flowers and leaves with black and random highlight with white. Steam. Glaze the upper side of the leaves with gum arabic solution.

Bunch together 2 or 3 flowers, buds and opening flowers and tie with binding wire at 'ground' level. Add 2 or 3 small leaves, facing inwards, around the bunch. Add 3 medium leaves and finally add 2 or 3 large leaves. Bind together and splay out a 'foot' so that the group will stand.

Blackthorn
Prunus spinosa

Spring-flowering blackthorn is found in hedgerows. The small, white, five-petalled flowers are filled with tiny reddish brown stamens, and the leaves open as the flowers begin to die.

REQUIREMENTS

- *White flower paste;* ● *brown tape;*
- *white cotton thread;* ● *30 and 33 gauge white wires;* ● *very small yellow stamens;* ● *small scissors;* ● *small 1 cm (³⁄₈") 5-petal blossom cutter;* ● *very small dog bone and ball tools;* ● *small 5-point star cutter;* ● *glue;* ● *light-green paste colour;* ● *cocktail stick (toothpick);* ● *miniature dog bone, ball and curved tools;* ● *baby sponge;*
- *needle-nose pliers;* ● *gum arabic solution;* ● *cornflour (cornstarch);*
- *dusting colours in moss-green, skin tone, black, white.*

1 STAMENS: Bind the thread around a finger 9 times, remove and pinch in the middle. Trim away loops that show while holding the opposite ones between the finger and thumb. Take 1 stamen and place about 1–2 mm (¹⁄₁₆") above the cut. Tie to a 30 gauge wire. Taper the threads at the base and tape. Splay out the stamens and paint the ends with skin tone dust and water.

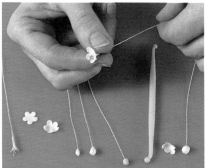

2 FLOWER: Cut out a 5-petalled blossom from very thin paste. Stretch and cup each petal with a very small dog bone tool. Apply glue to the tape just below the stamen threads and thread the flower on to the stamen wire. Cut in between the petals as far as possible. Dry upside down.

BUDS: Form small bud shapes in various sizes on to hooked 33 gauge wires. Inscribe petals on to the larger buds with a knife. For an opening bud, cut out a flower, stretch and cup. Dip a small bud in glue and mould the petals over it.

3 CALYX: Mix a small quantity of light leaf-green paste and roll out very thinly. Cut out a very small 5-pointed star. Reverse on the palm and stroke the points out with a very small curved tool or plastic cocktail stick. Place on a piece of sponge and press the centre with a very small ball tool and thread on to the wire. Draw up under the flower with the points between the flower petals and squeeze to secure. Make a calyx for each of the opening and larger buds too. For the smaller buds paint on the calyx with moss-green dust mixed with water.

COLOURING: Lightly dust the calyx and upper stem of the flowers and buds with moss/cornflour. Edge dust with black and random dust with white.

4 ASSEMBLY: The flowers and buds must be arranged all around the stem. Tape several small buds together with brown ⅓-width tape, gradually working down the stem. Add 2–3 larger buds; now add 1–2 opening buds spacing them out more; finally add 2–3 flowers. This is the main stem.

To make a thorny branch, take a 30 gauge wire and tape the top 1 cm (⅜″). Now add a bud, a larger bud, an opening bud and a flower. Tape this to the main stem. Make a second thorny branch and attach further down the main stem. Make several more, varying the arrangements. Allow the stem to thicken but trim if it becomes too cumbersome. Bend the stems for a natural effect, paint with black and steam. Finally, glaze with gum arabic solution.

WOOD ANEMONE

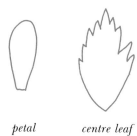

petal　　　*centre leaf*　　　*side leaf*

LESSER CELANDINE

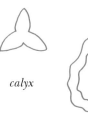

calyx

flower　　　　　　*leaves*

SWEET VIOLET

large lower petal　　*side/upper petal*

leaves　　　*calyx*

BLACKTHORN

flower　　　*calyx*

42

Woodland Flowers Scene

KEY TO THE DIAGRAM:

1 *25 cm (10") round cork mat*
2 *15 cm (6") thin cakeboard*
3 *log*
4 *7 stones*
5 *dead oak (14) and ivy (12) leaves*
6 *moss*
7 *3 stems of ivy*
8 *blackthorn tree with 12 flowers and 35 various buds*
9 *wood anemones with 4 flowers, 2 opening buds, and 9 groups of 3 leaves*
10 *violets with 6 flowers, 2 buds, and 4 small, 9 medium and 6 large leaves*
11 *celandines with 6 flowers, 1 opening bud, and 2 small, 5 medium and 3 large leaves.*

Composition

The oak-wood floor is scattered with decaying logs and leaves and, because it is so moist, moss grows in abundance. The cork base, mounted with a thin cakeboard, is covered with textured rolled fondant (sugarpaste) and painted with mottled browns and greens. The log is moulded from white, drying pastillage and painted. Moss is piped on with a fine tube and then painted light green. The log is positioned towards the back of the base with three stems of ivy arranged as if growing around the log.

A blackthorn tree grows from behind the log and gives height to the arrangement. In front of the log and blackthorn are the wood anemones. A plant of celandine grows on the right-hand side in front of the log and in the foreground are the violets. Stones and dead leaves are scattered to break the hard round line of the board.

Wayside Flowers

Many rural areas abound with·dry-stone walls and a profusion of wild flowers: blue meadow cranesbill, the distinctive trumpets of field bindweed, red campion in shades of light to dark pink, and lesser periwinkle.

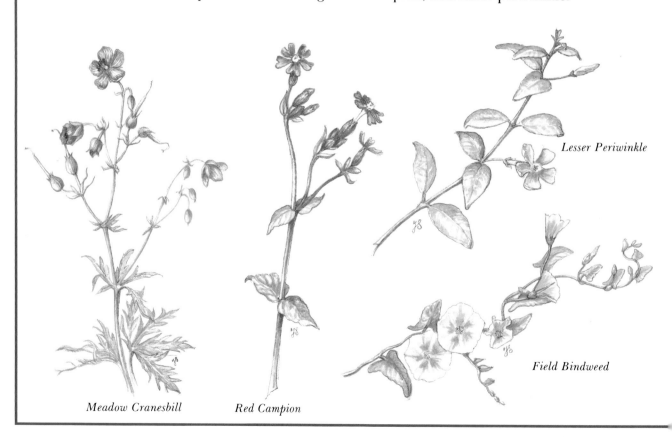

Lesser Periwinkle

Field Bindweed

Meadow Cranesbill

Red Campion

Retirement Cake

For a retirement cake with a walking theme, a corner is removed from an oblong cake to give the flowers 'growing' space. The cake is covered with light-green rolled fondant (sugarpaste) and the cakeboard flooded with the same-coloured royal icing. The mottled stones are made from lightly mixed white, blue, green and black rolled fondant and built around the cake starting from the base. Royal icing is piped on to the stones and border, and coloured with liquid colours to form moss and lichen. The flower sprays are positioned and arranged with stones, and secured with grass. For the final touch, a map and walking stick (made from flower paste) are placed by the cake.

THE FLOWER SPRAYS

- *2 meadow cranesbill flowers, 1 opening flower, 4 buds, 2 cranesbills, and 4 small and 4 large leaves*
- *2 red campion flowers, 1 opening flower, 11 buds, 1 dying flower, 1 seed pod, and 16 tiny, 4 small and 4 large leaves*
- *1 field bindweed flower, 1 opening flower, 5 buds and 1 seed pod*
- *2 periwinkle flowers, 1 opening flower, 1 bud, and 4 tiny, 6 small, 4 medium and 2 large leaves*

Meadow Cranesbill

Geranium pratense

This wild perennial geranium is a vivid cornflower-blue. The leaves are very serrated and the seed pods are shaped like cranes' bills – hence its popular name. It grows on verges in limestone areas throughout the summer.

REQUIREMENTS

● *White flower paste;* ● *small brown or black seedhead stamens;* ● *medium stamens;* ● *26 and 28 gauge white wire;* ● *white cotton thread;* ● *white stem tape;* ● *porcupine quill or plastic cocktail stick (toothpick);* ● *miniature dowel rolling pin;* ● *maple or geranium veiner;* ● *small calyx cutter;* ● *ball tool;* ● *palette (spatula) and modelling knives;* ● *fine sable brush;* ● *cupped moulds with holes;* ● *glue;* ● *dusting colours in black, white, rose-pink, cornflower-blue, violet, moss- and apple-green, lemon-yellow, skin tone.*

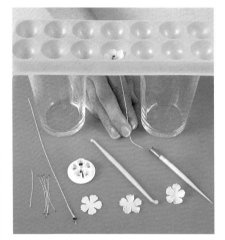

1 **STYLE:** Cut the head off a stamen. Soften the cotton end with water and flatten with a palette knife. Divide the end into several sections with a modelling knife and curl out. Colour light green.

STAMENS: Take 5 strands of stamens and fold the 10 heads level. Position the style 3 mm (⅛″) above the stamens

and tie to a 26 gauge wire, 5 mm (¼″) below the heads, with thread. Trim the threads and tape. Dust the threads with rose and paint the stamen heads black.

FLOWER: Cut out from thin paste and reverse. Roll a ball tool around the edges and slightly cup. Vein with a porcupine quill or plastic cocktail stick. Draw on to the wire and glue in place at the base of the stamen threads. Dry in a small cup mould with a hole for the wire, or hang upside down for a less open flower.

2 SEED POD: Prepare a style and tie to a 28 gauge wire so the tip protrudes 5 mm (¼″) above the wire; tape. Form a small ball of paste on to the wire, tapering the paste towards the style to make a cranesbill.

OPENING BUD: Mould a small ball of paste to a 26 gauge wire. Make a flower as in Step 1 and close over the ball with glue.

BUD: Mould a small egg-shaped

piece of paste on to a hooked 28 gauge wire. Take a short piece of stamen thread, fray the end and push into the top of the ball.

LEAVES: Make in three sizes using the insertion method (see Basic Techniques, page 11). Thin and stretch out the edges with a ball tool on the reverse side and place on the back of a leaf or veiner. Push the wire into the ridge, pinch the centre rib and dry.

3 COLOURING: Dust the flower with cornflower-blue and violet mixed with cornflour, then dust again with a little violet. Add a very small 5-petalled calyx, cupped, with the points between the petals. Dry and colour light green.

Add a small cupped 5-petalled calyx to the seed pods. Colour light green and over-dust with skin tone. Colour the opening buds as for the flower, add a calyx and colour light green. Dust the buds light green. Vein with a

small sable brush and paint with skin tone mixed with water. Over-dust the base with skin tone.

Dust the leaves with light moss/ lemon/cornflour on both sides. Over-dust the upper side with apple/ cornflower-blue/cornflour. Paint over the veins, removing the upper colour, with clean water. Dust the edges of the leaves with skin tone. Finally, edge dust all pieces with black and random dust with white.

4 ASSEMBLY: Take 2 green buds at slightly uneven levels and add a flower 1.5 cm (½″) above the buds. Add a small leaf 2.5 cm (1″) below the flower and tape together. Make groups in the same way using opening flowers and seed pods. Two groups may be taped together with a pair of large leaves where they join.

Red Campion

Silene dioica

Often found in woods and hedgerows growing with bluebells, red campion can range in colour from pale to bright pink. The five deeply cleft heart-shaped petals enclose a tiny white flower ruff that surrounds the stamens.

REQUIREMENTS

- *White flower paste;* ● *very small white stamens;* ● *campion or primrose cutter;* ● *very small 5-petal blossom plunger cutter;*
- *sponge;* ● *small scissors;*
- *knife;* ● *small paintbrush;*
- *cocktail stick (toothpick);*
- *maize (corn) husk;* ● *veiner;*
- *small ball tool;* ● *small hole tool;* ● *miniature dowel rolling pin;* ● *28 and 33 gauge white wire;* ● *white tape;* ● *white cotton thread;* ● *cornflour (cornstarch);*
- *glue;* ● *dusting colours in fuchsia-pink, cornflower-blue, black, moss-green, apple-green, red, brown, violet, white, lemon-yellow.*

1 STAMENS (STYLES): Group 5 stamen heads so they are level and tie to a 28 gauge wire with thread so the heads are about 5 mm (⅛″) above the wire; trim the threads. Bind with ⅓-width tape and paint light green.

INNER PETALS: Cut out from thin paste with a small 5-petal blossom plunger cutter and press into a sponge to cup. Thin the edges of the petals with a small ball tool. Thread on to the stamen wire and press into position so that the stamens just protrude. Dry upside down.

FLOWER: Make using the pedestal method (see Basic Techniques, page 11) and cut out. Make a small hole in the centre of the flower with a small hole tool. Cut into this to the centre separating the petals. A small 'V' can be trimmed from each petal to deepen the cleft with small scissors. Thin the petals with a small ball tool, slightly stretching outwards.

Dust the top and under side of the flower (but not the base) with fuchsia-pink mixed with cornflour and a little cornflower-blue. Lay on a piece of maize husk and press each petal, turning to align with the grain. Lightly cup the outer edges of the petals on the upper side for an opening flower and on the under side for a fully open flower.

Thread on to the stamen wire and roll and thin the stem of the flower with the first fingers, moulding it to the wire. Thin to a depth of 1 cm (⅜″) to allow for the calyx. Arrange the petals unevenly.

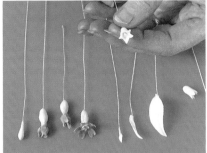

2 **CALYX:** Thread a tiny ball of paste on to the base of the flower stem. Mould a small piece of paste into a teardrop. Push the handle of a small paintbrush, dusted with cornflour, into the fat end and mould a tube about 1 cm (³⁄₈″) long; cut and thin. Remove from the handle and cut out 5 pointed petal shapes, about 3 mm (¹⁄₈″) deep, with scissors. Roll each petal with a cocktail stick and then groove. Hollow the inside with a small ball tool. Paint the base of the flower and the inside of the calyx petals with glue. Thread on and mould over the small ball of paste. Close the petals on to the flower base. A short length of the flower tube should show above the calyx. Slightly groove the calyx with the back of a knife and allow to dry.

3 **BUDS AND SEED BOXES:** Make in various sizes by moulding a small bullet shape to a hooked 33 gauge wire. For an opening bud, make a flower as in Step 1, omitting the stamens and inner petals. Close the petals in a spiral over the hooked wire and add a calyx. For a dying flower, make a flower and scrunch it up. Add a calyx with opening sepals. For the seed box, tie stamens to wire as before. Add a calyx with the petals curled outwards and squeeze in below these.

LEAVES: Make in 3 sizes using the insertion method (see Basic Techniques, page 11). Hold in the palm and thin the edges, place on a veiner, then insert a 33 gauge wire into the ridge. Crease the leaf along the central vein and allow the point to curve backwards.

5 **ASSEMBLY:** Tape together a group of 3 buds and tiny leaves, and group buds and opening flowers 2 cm (³⁄₄″) below these. Make a group of flowers, buds and tiny leaves and add about 4 cm (1½″) below the last group. Add a pair of medium leaves at the joint and a pair of large leaves further down the stem. Make other groups, using some dying flowers and seed pods. Dust the stems green then brown.

4 **COLOURING:** Carefully dust the flowers with fuchsia/blue/violet/cornflour to obtain a bright bluish pink. *Do not* discolour the white centre and flower tube. Dust the calyx with moss/lemon/cornflour mixed to a pale yellow-green. Dust the base with red/brown, add a little water and paint in lines towards the top. Paint the top pointed edges.

Colour the petals of the dying flower as for the flower, adding a little more blue/violet to the pink. Colour the calyx as above but browner. Dust the seed box light green and over-dust with brown; paint the stamens black and paint stripes in brown. Dust the buds light green, colouring the tips of some with pink; then lightly dust with brown and paint stripes.

Dust the small leaves with moss/brown/cornflour, then lightly dust the edges with brown. Dust the large and medium leaves all over with moss/lemon/cornflour, then over-dust the upper side with apple/moss/brown. Dust the edges with brown and paint in the veins with a fine sable brush and water.

Edge dust all pieces with black and random dust with white before steaming.

Field Bindweed

Convolvulus arvensis

A very common wayside and wasteland plant, the creeping and climbing field bindweed is a relative of the morning glory. Its pink trumpet unfolds to reveal a white five-point star. The binding stem has graduated arrow-shaped leaves.

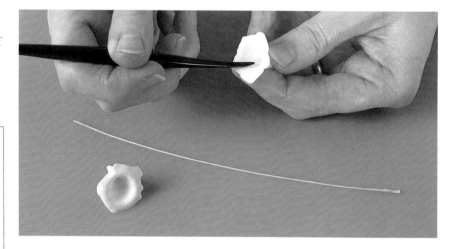

REQUIREMENTS

- *White flower paste;* ● *26, 28, 33 gauge wire;* ● *medium, pale yellow seedhead stamens;* ● *white cotton thread;* ● *tape;* ● *trumpet hollowing tool;* ● *small centre tool;* ● *fine grooving tool;* ● *miniature dowel rolling pin;* ● *5-point star calyx cutter;* ● *ball tool;* ● *sponge;* ● *cornflour (cornstarch);* ● *dusting colours in lemon-yellow, rose-pink, moss-green, apple-green, cornflower-blue, black, brown, white.*

---

1 STAMENS: Take 3 strands of stamens making 5 level heads. Remove the head from the sixth and place with another piece of cotton a little higher than the others. Tie to a 26 gauge wire so the stamens are 3 mm (⅛″) above the wire and tape. Paint with lemon mixed with water.

FLOWER: Make using the pedestal method starting from a medium teardrop (see Basic Techniques, page 11). Hollow the centre with a trumpet hollowing tool and, with the cone on the palm, thin the back of the petal edges and slightly hollow. Using a grooving tool, make two grooves from the centre out to each point 3 mm (⅛″) apart and pinch the ends. Pull the wire through with the stamens inside the trumpet. Trim the base to 2.5 cm (1″) and tighten to the wire with the first fingers. Dry upside down.

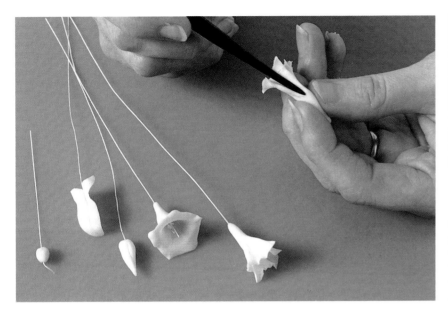

3 **COLOURING:** For the flowers, mix rose-pink dust with cornflour and add water to make a pale pink liquid and paint triangles between the 5 points of the flower. This will create a white 5-pointed star in the centre of the flower. Repeat on the outside. Add a little brown to the rose-pink and paint the white star on the outside of the flower. Paint opening buds and buds in pink.

Dust both sides of the leaves with moss/cornflour then over-dust the upper side with apple/cornflower-blue/cornflour. The smaller leaves should be lighter. Remove the dust on the veins with a sable brush and clear water. Edge dust all pieces with black and random dust with white.

2 **OPENING BUD:** Make as for the flower but do not hollow the edges. Pleat the flower around a hooked 26 gauge wire.

BUD: Form a flame shape and mould to a hooked 28 gauge wire. Mark with the back of knife 5 times and twist. Make in several sizes from 5 mm to 2 cm (¼–¾").

SEED POD: Take a 33 gauge wire and curl 1 cm (⅜") of one end around the tip of a paintbrush handle. Mould a small oval of paste just below the curve. Trim to a very short curl.

LEAVES: Make in 3 sizes using the insertion method (see Basic Techniques, page 11). Curl the leaves backwards; the smaller leaves should be less open.

4 **CALYX AND ASSEMBLY:** Cut a small 5-pointed star, stretch the points and hollow on a piece of sponge. Add to the base of the trumpet on flowers and buds with the points to the white lines and colour light green.

Take a tiny bud and add it to a small leaf. Add a pink bud and a medium leaf 1 cm (⅜") further down. Leave a larger space and add a flower with a large leaf. Make several groups, varying them with opening flowers and seed pods.

Lesser Periwinkle

Vinca minor

The periwinkle's five-petalled, blue-violet flowers spiral round in an anticlockwise direction. Short branch stems spread out from the main stem, usually carrying a single flower, and eventually root to form a dense ground cover.

REQUIREMENTS

- *White flower paste;* • *5-point star tool;* • *trumpet hollowing tool;*
- *small dowel rolling pin;* • *26 and 28 gauge white wire;* • *tiny white stamens;*
- *white cotton thread;* • *tape;* • *small ball tool;* • *wire strippers;* • *small sable brush;* • *small 5-point star calyx cutter;* • *rose-leaf veiner;* • *gum arabic solution;* • *cornflour (cornstarch);* • *dusting colours in cornflower-blue, violet, moss-, apple- and jade-green, brown, egg-yellow, black, white.*

1 STAMENS: Take 6 stamen heads and, keeping them level, tie to a 26 gauge wire. Tie close to the heads keeping them together and tape. Colour with egg-yellow.

FLOWER: Make using the pedestal method starting from a medium carrot shape (see Basic Techniques, page 11). Place the cutter over the cone in a *clockwise* direction. Shape the centre of the flower with a 5-point star tool so

that the ribs are to the centre of the petals. Open out more with the trumpet hollowing tool. Thin the edges and lightly cup each petal with a ball tool. Pinch the centre of each petal. Draw on to the stamen wire, pushing the stamens well inside the centre. Taper the cone of the flower to the stem with the first fingers. Arrange the petals to full or semi-open positions and dry.

2 **COLOURING THE FLOWER:** Mix cornflower-blue/violet/cornflour to produce a mid-blue/violet dust. Mix a little of the powder with water and paint the area surrounding the stamens and the 5-pointed star shape. Leave a very narrow white line all around this and continue colouring by brushing away from the line up the petals. Allow to dry. Dust the outside and inside of the flower with blue/violet. Dust the base of the flower with moss-green/cornflour.

3 **OPENING BUD:** Make as for the flower but mould on to a hooked 26 gauge wire and close the petals.

BUD: Mould a small candle-flame shape and make 5 indentations around it. Place on a hooked 26 gauge wire and twist slightly. Make in various sizes. Dust the tops of the buds with blue/violet and the bases with moss/cornflour.

CALYX: Cut out a small 5-pointed star from very thin paste. Pull out the points and attach to the base of the flowers and buds. Colour with moss/apple/cornflour.

LEAVES: Make several sizes in pairs using the insertion method (see Basic Techniques, page 11). Dust with moss/cornflour and a little apple-green. Dust the upper side only with jade-green. Paint away the dust with clean water to reveal the veining.

Edge dust all pieces with black and random dust with white before steaming. When dry, glaze the upper side of the leaves with gum arabic.

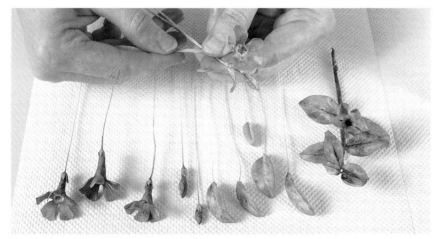

4 **ASSEMBLY:** Take a pair of small leaves and tape together. Add a medium-sized pair approximately 1 cm (³⁄₈″) below the first, then a second medium-sized pair with a flower a further 1 cm (³⁄₈″) down. Make a similar stem as above but with a bud or opening flower. Tape the two stems together with another large pair of leaves.

MEADOW CRANESBILL

 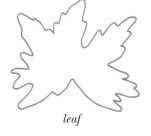  

leaf   *flower*   *calyx*

RED CAMPION

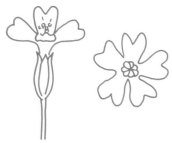  

flower centre

flower

leaves

FIELD BINDWEED

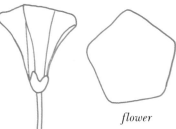   

calyx

flower   *leaves*

LESSER PERIWINKLE

 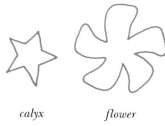 

calyx   *flower*

leaves

Wayside Flowers Scene

Composition

The stones for the wall are moulded from drying pastillage, then built into the wall using very little icing as adhesive. The piped moss growing between the stones helps to strengthen the structure. An old gatepost made from pastillage is attached to one end of the wall.

Meadow cranesbill are placed at the back of the arrangement with red campion on the right. The field bindweed is set creeping along the broken wall and periwinkle climbs up the gatepost. The ground is covered with grass, where a ladybird is seen crawling.

Pond Life

Plants and water have a special association. Above the surface, flowers and plants form moving reflections in the water and cast deep shadows where small waterbirds swim among their leaves. Below, in a hidden world, their stems form a maze concealing the silent fish.

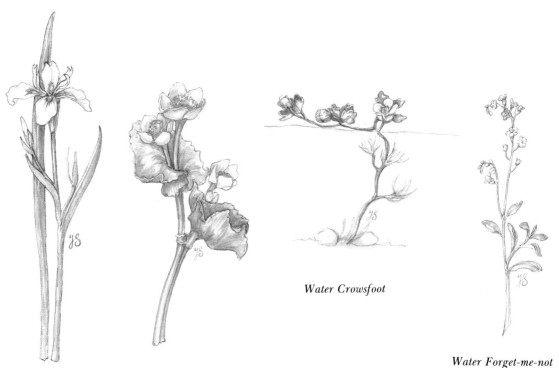

Water Crowsfoot

Water Forget-me-not

Marsh Marigold

Yellow Flag

B i r t h d a y   C a k e

The plaque, decorated with handpainted flowers, is made from rolled fondant (sugarpaste) mixed with gum tragacanth. The fish design is traced on to the cake sides and painted with brilliant white and then liquid colours. The cakeboard is flooded with royal icing coloured to match the cake covering, and the plaque is positioned on top of the cake. Piping jelly is mixed with pale green colour and brushed around the base and sides of the cake to give the effect of water.

THE FLOWER SPRAYS

- *1 yellow flag iris, 5 buds, and 12 leaves in various sizes*
- *2 march marigolds, 1 bud, and 3 small and 1 large leaves*
- *3 water forget-me-not flowers, 5 buds, 5 seed pods, and 4 small and 4 large leaves*
- *3 water crowsfoot flowers, 2 opening buds, 2 buds, and 7 groups of 5 leaves*

Yellow Flag

Iris pseudacorus

Yellow flag, a perennial inhabitant of marshes and the wet ground by ponds and rivers, always seems to grow just out of reach. Iris is the Greek word for rainbow; to the ancient Greeks it symbolized life and resurrection. This summer flower is related to the garden flag but comes only in yellow.

1 **LARGE PETAL (SEPALS):** Make using the insertion method (see Basic Techniques, page 11). Remove 3 mm (⅛″) of paper from a 33 gauge wire. Place the petal on the palm and thin the edges with a dog bone tool. Place on the veiner and press firmly. Reverse and place on the palm and lightly frill the outer edge of the petal with a small ball tool. Insert the wire into the ridge. Reverse. Press the insert area with a fine grooving tool and pinch to form a groove. The petal edges will curl upwards. For a more open flower, frill on the under side; the petal should roll backwards on the tip with the sides curling upwards. Mould a tiny ball of paste into a carrot shape, trim to 5 mm (¼″) long and stick into the groove at the base of the petal. Make 3 per flower.

SMALL PETAL: Using the insertion method (see Basic Techniques, page 11), cut out, and place on the palm and thin the edges with a very small dog bone tool. Reverse and hollow with a very small ball tool. Insert a 33 gauge wire. Make 3 per flower.

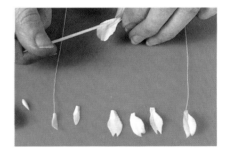

CRESTED STYLE: Using the insertion method, cut out, place on the palm and thin the edges. Fold in half lengthwise, place on the palm and hollow the upper part between the centre ridge and the edges, rolling the 'wings' backwards. Insert a 33 gauge wire. Mould a tiny carrot shape as for the sepal and attach at the base of the petal on the opposite side to the insertion ridge. Make 3 per flower.

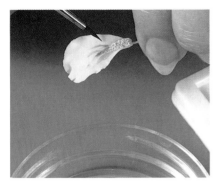

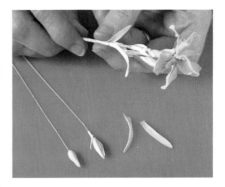

2 **COLOURING THE FLOWER:** Mix lemon-yellow, a touch of moss-green and cornflour and dust all the petals and buds. Moisten the 'carrot' at the base of the large and crested petals with a damp brush and sprinkle with semolina mixed with yellow dust to give the effect of pollen. Mix skin tone/brown with cornflour and water and paint fine radiating lines around the pollen 'carrot' on the large petal. Spot the pollen on the large and crested petals with the same colour.

3 **FLOWER ASSEMBLY:** Take the 3 crested petals, place with the curved ridges together and tie with thread. Place the 3 small petals between the crested petals, curving inwards, and tie. Bend the large petals backwards and place opposite each crested petal. Tie and tape the stem with ⅓-width tape.

4 **BUD:** Mould a small ball of paste into a flame shape. Push a hooked 26 gauge wire into the fat end and mould this to the wire. Press 3 grooves lengthwise around the bud with the back of a knife and twist. Make in various sizes.

LEAVES: Make using the insertion method as described for the snowdrop (see page 24).

OVARY: Mould a small ball of paste, thread up the stem and mould under the flower into a sausage shape. Press 3 grooves lengthwise down the ovary between the large petals with a fine grooving tool.

BUD SHEATH: Cut 2 small leaves from thin paste, vein on maize and wrap around the base of the bud. Add the other leaf a little down the stem. Tape the bud to a flower stem approximately 2 cm (¾″) below the ovary. Add a leaf over the joint. Join in a second bud but with larger leaves.

5 **FINAL COLOURING AND ASSEMBLY:** Mix moss/lemon/cornflour and dust the stem and leaves. Over-dust with apple/cornflour. Edge dust the flowers, stem and leaves with black and random dust with white. Steam and dry. Arrange a group of flowers and buds at different heights surrounded by leaves.

Marsh Marigold
Caltha palustris

The marsh marigold grows at fairly high altitudes and, as its name implies, on watery margins. There are five sepals, not petals, and fleshy, serrated, kidney-shaped leaves.

REQUIREMENTS
● *White flower paste;* ● *large pointed white or yellow stamens;* ● *very small white or yellow stamens;* ● *24, 28 and 33 gauge white wire;* ● *white cotton thread;* ● *white tape;* ● *small dowel rolling pin;* ● *maize (corn) husk;* ● *geranium veiner;* ● *cocktail stick (toothpick);* ● *ball tools;* ● *baby sponge;* ● *2 cm (³/₄″) five-petal blossom cutter;* ● *needle-nose pliers;* ● *cornflour (cornstarch);* ● *gum arabic solution;* ● *pencil;* ● *modelling knife;* ● *dusting colours in moss-green, lemon-yellow, egg-yellow, jade-green, apple-green, skin tone, black, white.*

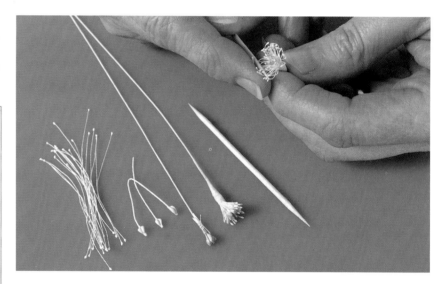

1 **STAMENS:** Take 3 large pointed yellow stamens and place tightly together to form a cone. Tie with thread to a half 24 gauge wire and trim. Dust with moss-green. Take a bunch of about 25 strands of very fine stamens with the heads fairly level, fold in half and hold them between the finger and thumb, splay out and thread the wire of the central core down through the middle so it is a little below the surrounding stamens. Bind with thread 1 cm (³/₈″) below the small stamens; taper the stamen thread. Curl the stamens towards the centre with a cocktail stick and bind with ¹/₃-width tape. Dust the stamens with lemon-yellow.

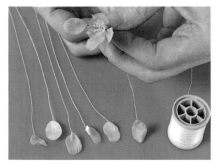

2 **SEPALS:** Using the insertion method (see Basic Techniques, page 11), form a ridge and cut out a sepal. Vein on a piece of maize husk. Thin the edges with a ball tool and insert a 33 gauge wire. Reverse and hollow the centre. For a more open flower, roll the top edges back on a cocktail stick and dry. Dust both sides of the sepals with lemon-yellow mixed with a touch of moss/egg-yellow/cornflour. Dust the lower part of the stems with moss/cornflour.

Bend the sepals back at 45 degrees with pliers. Place the sepals around the centre (see diagram, page 66), bind into position with thread and tape. Do not trim the wires as the flower has a thick stem. Dust the stem with moss and over-dust with skin tone. Steam.

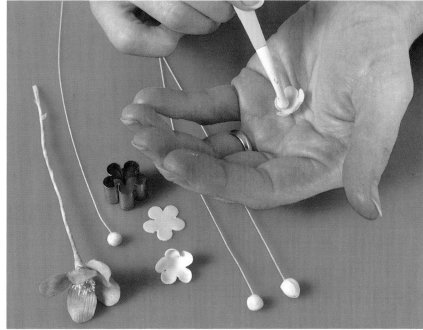

3 **BUD:** Mould a small pea-sized ball on to the end of a hooked 24 gauge wire. For a more developed bud, cut out with the 5-petal blossom cutter and add to the bud, enclosing the centre. Colour as for the flower.

LEAVES: Make in 3 sizes using the insertion method (see Basic Techniques, page 11). Cut out and vein on a geranium-type veiner. Thin and crinkle the edges with a small ball tool and insert a 28 gauge wire. Reverse and pinch the base on to the wire. Roll back the edges.

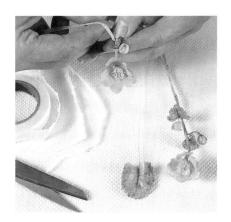

4 **FINAL COLOURING AND ASSEMBLY:** Dust the whole leaf with moss-green/cornflour. Over-dust the upper side with apple/jade/cornflour and then random dust with skin tone. Paint along the central vein to expose the under colour with clean water and then, working out from the vein, paint the radiating veins. With water added to the apple/jade mixture, spot paint a margin inside the outer edge. Dry. Steam, dry and then glaze with gum arabic solution.

Tape a flower and a bud with a small leaf at their junction 2.5 cm (1″) down the stem. The leaf should wrap around the stem. Add another flower or bud with a single leaf 2.5 cm (1″) below the first. Make a second group as above and tape them together with a large leaf at their junction. Colour the stems light green and over-dust with skin tone.

Water Forget-me-not

Myosotis scorpioides

This summertime flower grows by rivers, streams and ponds. The flowers are sky-blue and occasionally pink and are smaller than the garden variety. The stems unwind from a 'C' scroll as the flowers open.

REQUIREMENTS
- *White flower paste; ● small round-headed pale yellow stamens; ● 28 and 33 gauge white wire; ● white tape; ● small plunger 5-petal blossom cutter;*
- *cocktail sticks (toothpicks);*
- *very small ball tool; ● cornflour (cornstarch); ● glue; ● sponge;*
- *modelling knife; ● rose-leaf veiner; ● needle-nose pliers;*
- *wire strippers; ● dusting colours in lemon-yellow, cornflower-blue, blue-frost, moss- and apple-green, black, white.*

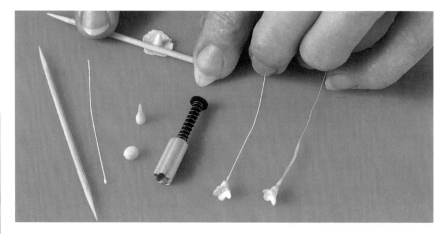

1 STAMEN: Using 1 stamen strand, remove one of the heads so there is a long thread. Paint pale green.

FLOWER: Make using the pedestal method (see Basic Techniques, page 11). Form a very small teardrop and roll out the base using a cocktail stick, keeping the pedestal very small. Cut out and push out gently with the plunger. Make a tiny hole in the centre of the flower with the point of a cocktail stick. Thin and hollow the petals with the ball tool. Thread the stamen through the flower, using a little glue under the stamen, and push the stamen level with the flower. Hold under the petals and roll to tighten with the first fingers. Trim the paste so that the base is no more than 3 mm (⅛″) deep.

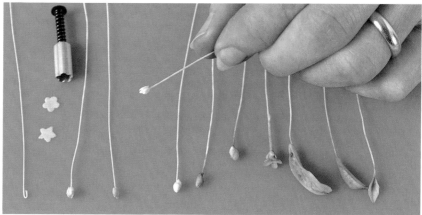

2 **COLOURING THE FLOWER:** Paint a fine ring of yellow in the centre of the flower around the stamen and allow to dry. Dust the flower with cornflower-blue mixed with a little blue-frost and quite a lot of cornflour to lighten the colour.

CALYX: Cut out a flower from flat paste with the plunger cutter and trim each petal to a point. Cup on a sponge and attach at the base of the flower. Dust the calyx and stem light green.

3 **BUDS:** Bend a tiny hook on a 33 gauge wire and mould a tiny bud on it. Dust blue.

SEPAL TUBE: Make as for the calyx but thread on to a hooked 33 gauge wire. Squeeze to the wire. Dust light green.

LEAVES: Make using the insertion method (see Basic Techniques, page 11). Make 3 in 3 sizes for each stem and pairs of the largest leaf for each 2-stem junction. Roll back the tip and

pinch. Dust both sides of the leaf with moss/cornflower-blue mixed with a touch of lemon. Add extra cornflour to obtain a pale green, add some apple-green and dust the upper leaf.

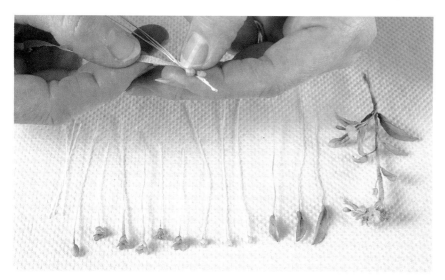

4 **FINAL COLOURING AND ASSEMBLY:** Edge dust the leaves, flowers and buds with black. Random dust the flowers and buds with white and the leaves with pale lemon. Steam and dry.

Bind 3–5 stamen heads at graduated levels to a bud with the bud below the stamens using ⅓-width tape. Add 2–3 more buds working down the stem. Now add 3–5 flowers, then 2–3 sepal tubes. Add a small leaf then the next-sized leaf below and opposite the first. Then add the third size leaf as before. Dust the stamens and stem light green. Curve the top of the stem. Make a small spray of leaves and add to the base of the flower stem, joining with a pair of the largest leaves.

Water Crowsfoot

Ranunculus aquatillis

A small member of the buttercup family, the water crowsfoot has two types of leaves: trefoil, toothed ones that float on the water; and fern-like ones beneath the surface. The five white petals surround a bright yellow centre.

REQUIREMENTS

● White flower paste; ● very small white stamens; ● 30 gauge wire; ● yellow and white cotton thread; ● white tape; ● 1.5 cm (¼") blossom cutter; ● small scissors; ● 5-point star cutter; ● binding wire; ● miniature dowel rolling pin; ● small geranium veiner; ● medium heart cutter; ● gooseberry-green paste colour; ● gum arabic solution; ● cornflour (cornstarch); ● dusting colours in moss-, apple- and jade-greens, black, white.

1 STAMENS: Place 4 stamen heads together and tie to a half 30 gauge wire. Trim the threads and paint with moss-green dust mixed with water. Wind the yellow thread around a finger 16 times. Cut the loops at one end straight across. Push the stamens into the middle so that the cut threads are a little above them. Tie, trim and tape with ⅓-width tape.

2 FLOWER: Cut out with a 5-petal blossom cutter. Thin the edges, stretch and ball the petals. Thread on to the stamen stem and stick just below the threads. Cut in between the petals with a small pair of scissors. Dry upside down.

3 **OPENING FLOWER:** Mould a small ball of paste on to a hooked 30 gauge wire. Cover completely with a blossom. To make a bud, mould a very small ball of paste on to a hooked 30 gauge wire.

CALYX: Colour some paste with gooseberry-green paste colour. Cut out a 5-pointed star and attach below the flower with the sepals between the petals. Add a calyx to each opening flower and bud.

LEAVES: Make using the insertion method (see Basic Techniques, page 11). Cut out with a medium heart cutter and trim a small triangle from each lobe. Vein, insert a short length of binding wire and squeeze at the base of the leaf.

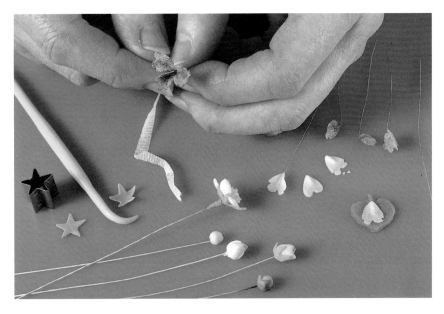

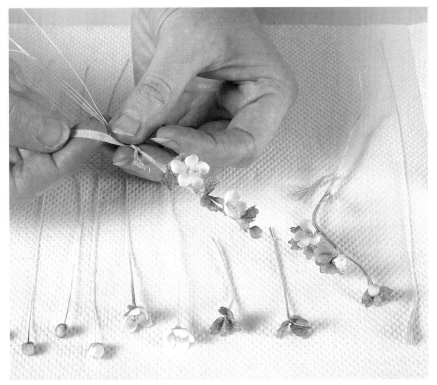

4 **FINAL COLOURING AND ASSEMBLY:** When dry, tape 3 leaves together to form a group. Dust the leaves, calyx and upper stems with moss/cornflour. Over-dust the upper side of the leaves with apple/jade/cornflour. Edge dust with black and random dust with white. Steam, then glaze the upper side of the leaves.

Tape a group of leaves 1 cm (⅜″) below a flower. Repeat with an opening flower and a bud. Tape the 3 groups together.

Make underwater leaves as follows: bind white thread 10 times around a finger and cut the loops. Tie to a 30 gauge wire, trim and tape. Dust with moss-green. Make 2–3 per stem and tape about 2 cm (¾″) below the upper leaves.

YELLOW FLAG

large petal *crested petal* *small petal*

leaves

MARSH MARIGOLD

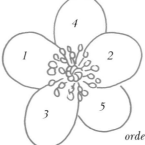 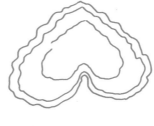 

order of petals *leaves* *petal* *calyx*

WATER FORGET-ME-NOT

leaves *flower* *calyx*

WATER CROWSFOOT

flower *calyx* *leaf*

Pond Flowers Scene

Composition

The old wooden cheese platter has a lovely water-effect grain. Through it are positioned three bolts: two are covered at the back with mud banks and the third is hidden inside the front clump of reeds. The 'water' is a shaped piece of perspex with brown/green tinted piping jelly smeared on both sides with a palette knife. The whole underwater scene is completed before the water is set in place. The pond bed and stones are made of rolled fondant (sugarpaste) painted a mud colour. The pastillage fish are mounted on wires with reeds to disguise them.

At the back, giving height to the arrangement, are yellow flag iris with groups of reed mace and bur reed on either side. On the left is a clump of water forget-me-not balanced with a spray of marsh marigolds on the opposite side. The water crowsfoot grows through holes drilled through the surface of the water for the stems. The clump of reeds in the foreground are made full length and then cut in half and matched up below and above the water line. Likewise, a mallard drake, modelled whole from pastillage, is cut in half so that its feet appear below the surface of the water.

Alpine Flowers

The majestic height, scenery and crisp air of the mountains are truly exhilarating, made perfect by the unexpected sight of tiny alpine flowers, of every colour, peeping through the snow.

Edelweiss

Alpine Primrose

Pasqueflower

Trumpet Gentian

Graduation Cake

This mountain cake would be ideal to celebrate a career promotion or a graduation. Rolled fondant (sugarpaste) is used to cover the cake and to make the foothills, and is textured by pummelling. It is also used to mould the rocks, but is allowed to dry a little to obtain a crusty, rocky effect. The cakeboard is flooded with let-down royal icing. The flower sprays are positioned and attached with royal icing. The stream is painted on with coloured piping jelly. Finally, the snow areas are brushed with clean water and sprinkled with castor (superfine) sugar.

THE FLOWER SPRAYS

- *4 alpine primroses, 2 opening flowers, 6 buds, and 3 small, 3 medium and 4 large leaves*
- *4 pasqueflowers, 1 bud and 3 groups of 3 leaves*
- *2 trumpet gentian, 1 opening flower, 1 bud and 3 leaf rosettes*
- *3 edelweiss with 4 leaf rosettes*

Edelweiss

Leontopodium alpinum

A mountain flower, edelweiss also grows well in alpine and rock gardens. The spear-shaped leaves are woolly in appearance and the flower consists of a cluster of yellow heads surrounded by a rosette of tightly packed bract-like leaves that are snow white. The edelweiss is now a protected flower as a result of over-picking.

REQUIREMENTS

● *White flower paste;* ● *edelweiss (or daisy) cutter;* ● *33 gauge white wire;*
● *small snowdrop cutter;* ● *white tape;*
● *semolina;* ● *cornflour (cornstarch);*
● *white vegetable fat;* ● *modelling knife;* ● *glue;* ● *very small yellow stamens;* ● *white cotton thread;*
● *porcupine quill or plastic cocktail stick (toothpick);* ● *small ball tool;*
● *castor (superfine) sugar;* ● *dusting colours in apple-green, lemon-yellow, cornflower-blue, silver, black, white.*

1 CENTRES: Mould tiny balls of paste to hooked wires. Dip in glue, then in semolina mixed with yellow dust. Dry.

STAMENS: Arrange about 10 stamens around each centre (and slightly above it), tie with thread and tape.

2 **PETALS:** Roll paste thinly and cut out 3- and 4-petalled florets. Reverse on the palm and hollow and stretch the under side with a small ball tool. Reverse and indent a central groove down each petal with a porcupine quill or cocktail stick. Apply a little glue at the base and stick on to less than one half of the centre ball. Pinch on to the stem just below the ball. Pull and roll back the petals. Make 3–4 of these groups per flower. Dry upside down.

3 **FLOWER ASSEMBLY:** Cluster 3–4 groups of petals around 2–3 centres to form the flowers. Tie with thread and tape. Add 5–6 small alternating leaves down each stem.

4 **LEAF ROSETTES:** Mould a small 'candle' of paste on to a wire. Make 2 small cuts dividing it into 3. Mould the 2 outer sections into small leaves with a central bud. Using a small snowdrop cutter, add 2 sets of 3 leaves, then add 2–3 single leaves as on the stems of the flowers. Mould some extra single leaves with 2 sizes of leaf using the insertion method (see Basic Techniques, page 11).

5 **COLOURING AND ASSEMBLY:** Dust the leaves, stems and rosettes with apple/lemon/cornflour. Dust a second time with cornflower-blue added to the mixture. Random dust all leaves with silver and the flowers with white. Edge dust with black, steam and dry. Lightly moisten the foliage with a brush and sprinkle with castor sugar.

Make groups of flowers and rosettes of leaves with the single leaves growing out from the base.

Trumpet Gentian

Gentiana acaulis

This gentian is a bright metallic blue with black markings inside the trumpet, and is very low growing with hardly any stem. Attractive rosettes of leaves surround the flowers.

REQUIREMENTS
● *White flower paste;* ● *small star cutter;* ● *very small beige/cream stamens;* ● *white cotton thread;* ● *glue;* ● *cornflour (cornstarch);* ● *28 and 26 gauge white wire;* ● *stem tape;* ● *cocktail stick (toothpick); small sable paintbrush;* ● *small dowel rolling pin;* ● *ball tool;* ● *modelling knife;* ● *trumpet hollowing tool;* ● *fine grooving tool;* ● *dusting colours in black, cornflower-blue, ice-blue, violet, lemon-yellow, moss-green, apple-green, white.*

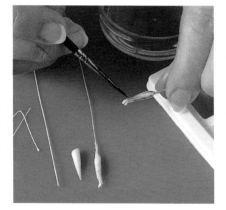

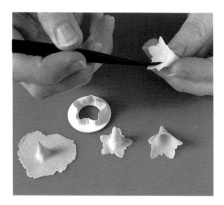

1 STAMENS: Lay 3 strands of stamens side by side and glue the threads together, leaving just the heads free. When dry, fold in half (level) to form 2 groups of 3 heads, tie to a 26 gauge wire with thread and tape. Add a small carrot-shaped piece of paste with a flat base so the point is below the stamens. Paint with stripes of black.

2 FLOWER: Make using the pedestal method (see Basic Techniques, page 11) and a medium teardrop of paste. Hollow out the centre using a trumpet hollowing tool. Make a central groove down the petals with a fine grooving tool. Pinch on the outside to form a ridge. Push in a groove between the petals to pleat the flower. Curl out the more open flowers on a cocktail stick.

3 **COLOURING THE FLOWER:** Dust the inside of the flowers with cornflower/ice-blue mixed with a little violet and a little cornflour to lighten. Push the stamen wire through so that the stamens are inside the trumpet. When dry, dust the rest of the flower as above and paint black streaks in the centre with liquid colour.

4 **CALYX:** Make using the pedestal method and a small star cutter. Groove as for the flower and attach to the base.

FLOWER STEM LEAVES: Using the smallest leaf template, cut out a pair of leaves from flat paste. Hollow on the under side, reverse and groove down the centres. Attach just below the calyx. Add another pair a little below but alternating.

ROSETTES OF LEAVES: Using the smallest leaf template, cut out and push a 28 gauge wire through the centre of the leaf. Moisten inside and sandwich together enclosing the end of the wire. Dry. Cut out another pair of the smallest leaves, hollow and fold through the centre lengthwise. Attach either side of the central leaves. Add 2 more pairs of alternating larger leaves.

BUD: Mould a candle-flame shape and mark petals down its length with the back of a knife. Open out a little at the point and twist slightly. Add a calyx and colour as for the flower.

5 **COLOURING AND ASSEMBLY:** Dust the calyx and leaves with moss-green/cornflour and then apple-green/lemon-yellow.

Assemble the flowers, buds and rosettes in small groups.

Alpine Primrose
P r i m u l a   r o s e a

There are a number of mountain primroses that look very similar. The flowers are like native primroses but the mountain varieties have more succulent leaves. Most of the alpine primroses are protected by law.

REQUIREMENTS
● *White flower paste;* ● *tiny yellow stamens;* ● *28 and 33 gauge white wire;* ● *tape;* ● *white cotton thread;* ● *miniature dowel rolling pin;* ● *small primrose cutter;* ● *scissors;* ● *small centre tool;* ● *modelling knife;* ● *miniature ball tool;* ● *rose-leaf veiner;* ● *binding wire;* ● *glue;* ● *cornflour (cornstarch);* ● *cocktail stick (toothpick);* ● *gum arabic solution;* ● *dusting colours in lemon-yellow, fuchsia-pink, violet, moss-green, cornflower-blue.*

1 STAMENS: Hold 3 stamen heads level, place a 33 gauge wire just under the heads and tie with thread. Bind with ⅓-width tape. Paint with moss-green mixed with water.

FLOWER: Make using the pedestal method (see Basic Techniques, page 11) and a pea-sized piece of paste rolled into a carrot shape with a fine point. Cut out with a small primrose cutter. Push a small centre tool into the centre to make a small hole. Cut between the petals with scissors to near the centre hole. Use the back of a knife to score a gully from the centre down the length of each petal. Hollow and

push out each side of this with a small ball tool. Pull the stamen wire through the centre until the stamens are level with the flower. With the first fingers, roll the under side of the flower to thin and tighten. Trim the base to 1 cm (⅜″). The stamens should be inside the flower but still visible.

2 COLOURING THE FLOWER: Paint the star-shaped centre with water or alcohol mixed with lemon-yellow. Dry. Dust the flower tube with lemon/cornflour then dust both sides of the flower with fuchsia/violet/cornflour to produce a magenta-pink. Do not dust the yellow centres.

3 **CALYX:** Mould a small ball of paste into a thin cigar shape and trim one end flat. Insert a blunt-ended cocktail stick into one end of the paste and mould into a tube, keeping the other end pointed. Trim to a length of 1 cm (⅜″) and remove the stick with a twist. Make five small equal cuts around the rim with small scissors. Cut away triangles to leave 5 points. Press into the centre of each sepal with the pointed end of the cocktail stick to thin. Pinch and pull gently to lengthen. Moisten the base of the flower tube, draw the calyx up the stem and mould to the flower tube. Make lengthwise grooves between the sepals with the back of a knife.

4 **OPENING FLOWERS:** Make as for the flower in Step 1 and insert a hooked 33 gauge wire. Paint the petals with glue and close together. Colour as for the under side of the flower.

BUD: Mould a small piece of paste into a carrot shape and insert a hooked 33 gauge wire at the pointed end. Roll between the first fingers to tighten. The top should be bulbous with a rounded point. Colour as for the under side of the flower.

LEAVES: Make using the insertion method (see Basic Techniques, page 11) and insert a 28 gauge wire. To colour the leaves and calyx, mix moss-green with a touch of cornflower-blue/cornflour and dust both sides of the leaf, the stem and calyx. Add more cornflower-blue to the mix and over-dust the upper side of the leaf. Paint the veins with clean water. Steam and glaze.

ASSEMBLY: Bunch together several flowers, opening flowers and buds with the bud slightly lower. Tape just below the calyxes, but do not trim the wires away. Make several varying groups. Hold at 'ground' level – 5–8 cm (2–3″) from the top flowers. Surround with leaves – the small ones inside and the large outside. Tie together with binding wire. Dust the stems light green.

Pasqueflower

P u l s a t i l l a   v u l g a r i s

The beautiful pasqueflower, a relative of the anemone, can still be seen in chalky pastureland, and is often cultivated in rock gardens. The six sepals are bell-shaped with a ruff of feathery, hairy leaves. The leaves are very divided and appear as the violet flowers fade.

REQUIREMENTS

● *White flower paste;* ● *bright violet cotton thread;* ● *white cotton thread;* ● *24 and 28 gauge wire;* ● *medium seedhead pale yellow stamens;* ● *white tape;* ● *cornflour (cornstarch);* ● *maize (corn) husk;* ● *small cupped mould with a hole;* ● *large and small ball tools;* ● *dog bone tool;* ● *maple veiner;* ● *miniature dowel rolling pin;* ● *sponge;* ● *binding wire;* ● *wire strippers;* ● *small needle-nose pliers;* ● *sugar;* ● *glue;* ● *dusting colours in violet, cornflower-blue, moss- and apple-green, black, white.*

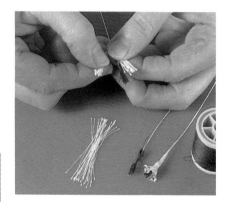

1 **STAMENS:** Wind the violet thread around a finger 15 times, remove and fold in half. Position a 24 gauge wire so the end of the wire is halfway up the loops. Tie with thread and trim to a point. Lay 25 strands of stamens, with the heads level, on the work surface. Place the centre wire in the middle of the stamens about 1 cm (⅜″) below the point. Turn and fold rest of the stamens up level on the opposite side of the centre. Bind with white thread 1 cm (⅜″) below the point. Trim and tape.

2 **FLOWER:** Cut 2 sets of 3-petalled shapes from very thin paste. Keep one covered. Place the other one on the palm, thin the edges and stretch each petal. Vein each petal on maize. Reverse on the palm and ball inside the tips to roll back. Place into a small cup mould, pressing in with a large ball tool. Make the second group of petals and place over the first with alternated petals; moisten to stick together. Thread the stamen wire through the centre, stick with glue and allow to dry.

3 **OPENING FLOWER:** Cut out as for the flower, thin the edges and reverse to vein. Place in the mould, add the second set of petals and insert the stamens. Close the petals and hang upside down to dry. For a bud, mould a small pea-sized piece of paste into an oval and attach to a hooked 24 gauge wire. Cut out a set of 3 petals, thin the edges and hollow. Close around the centre. Dust the flowers and buds with violet/cornflower-blue/cornflour.

RUFF: Cut out the ruff from thin paste. Push out towards the edges with a small ball tool to stretch and curl. Place on a piece of sponge and push into it with a large ball tool. Paint the stem 1 cm (3/8″) below the flower with glue. Thread the ruff up the stem and squash to the stem. Moisten the upper side of the ruff and wrap the ruff well around the buds.

4 **LEAVES:** Make using the insertion method (see Basic Techniques, page 11). Thin the edges vigorously with a dog bone tool. Vein, reverse and curl the edges with a small ball tool (on the veined side). Reverse to insert the wire. On the right side, pinch along the veins to give a crinkled effect. A smaller pair of leaves can be cut out from the main leaf.

Dust the leaves, ruffs and stems with moss/cornflour. Dust the upper leaf with apple/cornflower-blue/cornflour. Over-dust the ruff with the apple mixture. Paint along the leaf veins with clean water to reveal the under colour. Edge dust flowers, ruffs and leaves with black and random dust with white. Steam.

5 **ASSEMBLY:** Take a pair of smaller leaves, bend the wire close to the leaves at right angles and tape a large leaf 3 mm (1/4″) below. Make a bunch of 2–3 open flowers, 2 opening flowers and a bud. The open flowers should be highest. Bind with wire at 'ground' level. Surround with 3–4 groups of leaves. Trim the wires to form a stand.

To achieve the furry effect on the under side of the leaves and ruff, paint the surfaces with water and sprinkle with sugar.

EDELWEISS

flower   *3-leaf group*   *single leaves*

TRUMPET GENTIAN

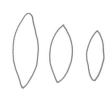

calyx   *flower*   *leaves*

ALPINE PRIMROSE

flower

leaves

PASQUEFLOWER

ruff   *flower*   *leaf*

Alpine Mountain Scene

Composition

The mountains are a right angle of plywood covered with white rolled fondant (sugarpaste) and textured with modelling tools. The foothills are cut from polystyrene to lighten the weight and covered with rolled fondant (sugarpaste). The stream is made from piping jelly, coloured light blue/grey and painted on. It cascades down the mountain over rolled fondant (sugarpaste) rocks and pebbles in the foreground.

The ermine (or stoat) with a creamy white winter coat and a black-tipped tail was moulded from pastillage and furred with a small nozzle and royal icing. A dipper stands on a stone in the stream.

To create distance, the smaller flowers (alpine primrose) are set at the back growing from crevices in the rocks. The edelweiss is by the stream near the centre with a smaller plant on the right-hand side. Trumpet gentian nestle under the rocks in the foreground and the pasqueflower grows on the right. Grass, made from piped royal icing, emerges from under the snow and ferns are piped on to wire.

Seashore Flowers

Looking for life in rock pools is all part of enjoying the seaside. Seashore flowers are found growing in the crevices of cliffs and rocks and the gentler slopes of sand dunes: spiky blue-green sea holly, white sea campion, pretty pink thrift and trumpet-shaped sea bindweed.

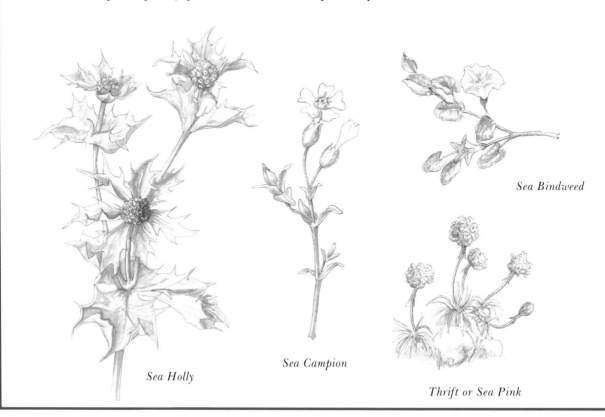

Sea Bindweed

Sea Holly

Sea Campion

Thrift or Sea Pink

Summer Birthday Cake

One side of this oval cake has been sloped to provide a background for the sea, which appears to recede into the distance. This design could also be used for a 'Bon Voyage' or, indeed, a 'Welcome Home' cake. It is covered with pale blue rolled fondant (sugarpaste), and the cakeboard is flooded with let-down royal icing in a sand colour. The birds are traced on the cake and painted with brilliant white and liquid colours. The tiny sea creatures are made from flower paste and coloured. The sprays of flowers are supported between the moulded rocks and secured with royal icing. Grass is piped between the rocks and coloured, and the shellfish are positioned in the pool area. Coloured piping jelly is piped to form waves and painted around the board and over the sloped cake background. More jelly is heated and poured into the pool area. Semolina is finally sprinkled over the rocks and the edge of the sea for sand.

THE FLOWER SPRAYS

- *3 stems of sea holly*
- *2 sea campion, 1 opening bud, 1 bud and 2 leaf rosettes*
- *1 sea bindweed, 1 opening bud, 1 bud, and 2 small, 4 medium and 2 large leaves*

Sea Holly

E r y n g i u m   m a r i t i m u m

Not at all related to the holly but surprisingly to the carrot family, this beautiful architectural plant grows in sand and shingle by the sea. The flowers are a blue-green colour with spiky bracts of pale silver-green.

REQUIREMENTS

● *White flower paste;* ● *small white round-head stamens;* ● *white cotton thread;* ● *white tape;* ● *30 and 24 gauge white wire;* ● *small plunger 5-petal blossom cutter;* ● *cocktail stick (toothpick);* ● *baby sponge;* ● *egg white;* ● *rose-leaf veiner;* ● *fine grooving tool;* ● *miniature dowel rolling pin;* ● *dog bone tool;* ● *wire strippers;* ● *cornflour (cornstarch);* ● *dusting colours in moss-green, blue-frost, cornflower-blue, red, silver, black, white.*

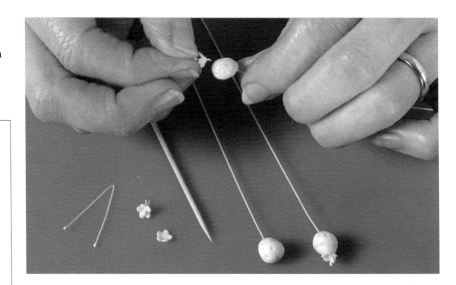

1 **FLOWER:** Mould a large pea-sized ball of paste and push on to a hooked 24 gauge wire. Make holes, 3 mm (⅛″) apart, all over the ball with a cocktail stick. Dip in egg white. Roll out some paste very thinly, cut out a small blossom and push it into a piece of sponge to cup. Fold a strand of stamens in half. Hold the heads between the finger and thumb and cut off the base so the stamens are only 5 mm (¼″) long. Push them through the centre of the flower and push the whole into a hole in the ball. Repeat, covering the ball (except for the base) with 10–12 florets. Make several in varying sizes.

2 LEAF: Make using the insertion method (see Basic Techniques, page 11) and 30 gauge wire. Press on to a rose-leaf veiner. Reverse and draw a fine grooving tool out at each point of the leaf to lengthen and slightly ridge. Reverse, with the insertion ridge uppermost, and insert the wire. Reverse and crease down the central vein. Groove the upper side of the leaf base with the grooving tool. Pinch each point and dry with the point bending back a little.

Make 7 leaves (bracts) to surround each flower, small for small and medium for larger flowers. Make 3 leaves for each flower stem, large for large and medium for small flowers.

3 COLOURING: Mix moss/silver/blue-frost/cornflour to make a pale green-silver colour and dust the flower. Over-dust with cornflower-blue and a touch of red/cornflour. Dust the leaves with the green-silver mix and over-dust the upper sides with silver.

ASSEMBLING THE FLOWERS: Bend the wire at right angles to the 7 surrounding leaves (bracts); arrange the leaves around the flower and tie with thread. Bend the wires of the 3 larger leaves in the same way. Tape down the stem 1–2 cm (⅜–½″) and tape in the 3 larger leaves.

4 LARGE THREE-PIECE LEAF: Cut out and thin edges with a dog bone tool and flute with a cocktail stick. Squeeze on to the stem about 3 cm (1″) below the other leaves. Dry upside down. Colour as for the other leaves.

5 ASSEMBLY: Edge dust all the leaves and flowers with black and random dust with white. Steam. Arrange stems in groups of 2 to 4 growing in crevices of sugarpaste rocks.

Sea Campion

Silene maritima

The white sea campion is to be found on cliffs and shingle by the sea. It has a particularly attractive bladder-shaped calyx in soft green and terracotta. The leaves and leaf buds form a thick carpet beneath the flowers.

REQUIREMENTS
- *White flower paste;* • *small brown- or black-headed stamens with white cottons;* • *26 and 28 gauge wire;* • *tape;* • *white cotton thread;* • *scissors;* • *small ball tool;* • *medium primrose cutter;*
- *miniature dowel rolling pin;*
- *trumpet hollowing tool;*
- *modelling knife;* • *cornflour (cornstarch);* • *dog bone tool;*
- *small sable brush;* • *small snowdrop cutter;* • *dusting colours in moss-green, lemon-yellow, skin tone, apple-green, black, white.*

1 **STAMENS:** Lay 3 × 2.5 cm (1″) lengths of thread together and tie to a half 26 gauge wire so they lie 1 cm (⅜″) above the wire. Trim below the tie. Take 8 stamen heads and place 3 mm (⅛″) below the top of the threads. Tie, trim and tape with ⅓-width tape.

FLOWER: Make using the pedestal method (see Basic Techniques, page 11) from a 1 cm (⅜″) ball of paste. Cut out with a primrose cutter. Hollow the centre with a trumpet hollowing tool. Cut between the petals towards the centre to separate. Hollow the petals with a small ball tool and indent the centres with the back of a modelling knife. Thread the stamen wire through the flower with the stamens standing above.

84

2 **BUDS:** Make an opening bud as for the flower but mount on a hooked 26 gauge wire and close the petals together. For a bud, mould a small candle-flame shape and mount on a 26 gauge wire.

CALYX: When the flower is dry, lightly dust the base and inside of the tube with moss-green/cornflour. Mould a small ball of paste to the base of the flower tube. Take a pea-sized ball of paste and mould over the small end of a dog bone tool; trim to 1 cm (⅜″) and remove from the tool. Divide into 5 with cuts 3 mm (⅛″) deep. Cut away to form 5 points. Thin these by pressing between the finger and thumb. Pull the calyx over the ball at the flower base, maintaining the bladder shape. Mould the points to the flower tube.

3 **COLOURING:** Mix moss/lemon/ cornflour into a pale yellow-green and dust the calyxes, leaf buds and upper stems. Mix skin tone with water and paint fine lines and dots on the calyx. When dry, lightly over-dust with the same colour.

Add more moss to the yellow-green mixture and dust the leaves. Add apple-green and over-dust the upper side of the leaves. Edge dust all pieces with black, random dust with white.

4 **LEAF BUD AND LEAVES:** Mould a small flame shape on to a 28 gauge wire. Cut out a medium snowdrop petal and mould around the bud. Cut a pair of small leaves from thin paste, thin the edges and crease lengthwise. Moisten the base and attach to the stem just below the bud; add the second pair opposite. Dry and repeat with another pair just below, alternating. Make groups with larger buds and leaves.

5 **ASSEMBLY:** Tape a bud 2 cm (¾″) down the stem of a flower. Add a small leaf group and then another flower or opening bud with a larger leaf group. Add pairs of leaves at the junctions by moulding directly on to the stem. Colour when dry, then steam.

Sea Bindweed

Calystegia soldanella

The flower of the sea bindweed looks similar to the field variety but the leaves are quite different: they are fleshy and kidney-shaped compared to the arrow shape of the latter. The sea bindweed flowers on coastal sand in high summer.

REQUIREMENTS
- *White flower paste;* • *medium seedhead yellow stamens;* • *30 and 26 gauge wire;* • *tape;*
- *white cotton thread;* • *cornflour (cornstarch);* • *small 5-petal blossom cutter;* • *trumpet hollowing tool;* • *fine grooving tool;* • *cocktail stick (toothpick);*
- *miniature dowel rolling pin;*
- *wire strippers;* • *gum arabic solution;* • *dusting colours in fuchsia-pink, cornflower-blue, moss- and apple-green, black, white.*

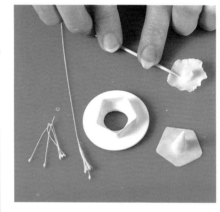

1 **STAMENS:** Place 5 stamen heads level with a sixth head 3 mm (1/8″) above them, and tie with thread to a 26 gauge wire and tape.

FLOWER: Make using the pedestal method and a medium teardrop of paste (see Basic Techniques, page 11). Lightly frill the edge with a cocktail stick. Place on the palm and hollow inside the edge. Hollow the centre with a trumpet hollowing tool. Using the fine grooving tool, make two grooves 3 mm (1/8″) apart coming out to each point and pinch the ends; also mark grooves halfway between these. Roll back the flower edges. Insert the wire with the stamens inside the trumpet and tighten the base of the flower to it. Make some smaller flowers that are less open.

2 **COLOURING THE FLOWER:** Mix fuchsia-pink, a touch of cornflower-blue and cornflour. Add water and paint triangles between the flower points with a fine sable brush. This will produce a white star. Paint over the same area on the outside.

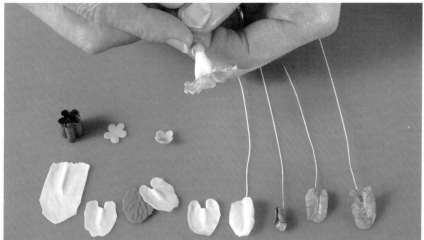

3 **OPENING BUD:** Make a smaller flower as in Step 1 but attach to a hooked 26 gauge wire; pleat the flower around it. Colour as for the flower.

BUD: Mould a small ball of paste into a flame shape and push a hooked 26 gauge wire into the fat end. Mark lengthwise around it with the back of a knife. Twist slightly.

4 **LEAF:** Make in three sizes using the insertion method (see Basic Techniques, page 11) and 30 gauge wire.

To make the calyx, cut out a blossom from thin light-green paste and close tightly around the base of the flowers and buds.

Dust both sides of the leaves with apple/moss/cornflour mixed with a touch of cornflower-blue. Add more cornflower-blue to the mix and use to over-dust the upper side of the leaf and to dust the calyx and the stems. Edge dust with black and random dust with white. Steam and dry. Glaze the upper side of the leaves with gum arabic solution and allow to dry.

5 **ASSEMBLY:** Tape a medium leaf about 1 cm (⅜″) below a small leaf. Add a bud and another medium leaf, then a flower. Make a second stem with an opening bud. Tape the stems together with 2 large leaves.

Thrift or Sea Pink

Armeria maritima

Walks over rocks, cliff tops and dunes will often lead to the discovery of this pretty pink ball of tiny florets, set on stems above cushions of fringe-like leaves. It can also be found in the mountains.

REQUIREMENTS

● *White flower paste;* ● *very small white stamens;* ● *24 and 33 gauge white wire;* ● *tape;* ● *small plunger 5-petal blossom cutter;* ● *very small ball and dog bone tools;* ● *1.5 cm (¼") rose calyx cutter;* ● *2 cm (¾") daisy cutter;* ● *cocktail stick (toothpick);* ● *scientific wire;* ● *white cotton thread;* ● *small 5-point star cutter;* ● *cornflour (cornstarch);* ● *dusting colours in moss-green, rose-pink, fuchsia-pink, cornflower-blue, violet, skin tone, black, white.*

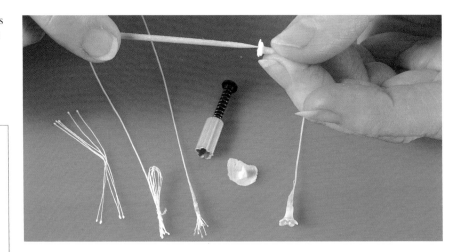

1 STAMENS: Take 5 strands of stamens and fold so that the 10 heads are level. Place a short length of 33 gauge wire 3 mm (⅛") below the heads and tie. Trim the ends and tape with ⅓-width tape. Splay out 5 of the stamens and cut off the heads of the 5 remaining in the centre. Paint the heads light green.

FLOWER HEADS: Make using the pedestal method (see Basic

Techniques, page 11) from a very small ball of paste. Cut out the flower with the plunger cutter. Make a small hole in the flower centre with a cocktail stick. Thin and cup the petals with the ball tool. Thread the stamen wire through the centre with the stamens above the flower. Thin the flower tube by rolling between the first fingers. Trim to 5 mm (¼").

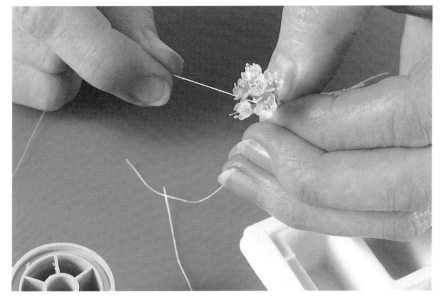

3 **CALYX:** Cut out 2 5-petalled rose calyxes from thin paste. Push out the sepals with a dog bone tool to lengthen and cup. Thread one on to the stem and mould to the base of the flower, then the other alternating to give a 10-sepalled calyx.

2 **COLOURING THE FLOWERS:** Mix rose-pink with quite a lot of cornflour to lighten. Add a touch of violet and cornflower-blue to make a pale bluish pink. Dust the florets on the outside only so that the stamen threads stay white. Over-dust with fuchsia-pink. Form posies of 5–9 florets and tape together.

4 **LEAVES:** Cut out a calyx and divide each sepal into 3 or 4. Place on the palm and push out with a dog bone tool. Thread on to the stem 2–3 cm (¾″) below the flower and tighten. Cut out two small daisies and divide and tool as above. Add to the first leaf but reverse so that the leaves curl down. Another set can also be added . Mould a small ball of paste underneath to form a cushion.

LEAF CUSHIONS: Make a hook in a 24 gauge wire. Make the first leaf set as above but squeeze it over the hook. Dry. Make two daisy leaves, stick together with a ball of paste underneath and thread on to the centre so that they curl downwards.

5 **COLOURING AND ASSEMBLY:** Dust the calyx, leaves and stems with a mix of moss/cornflower-blue/cornflour. Over-dust the base of the leaf cushions with skin tone.

Make opening flowers from flat paste. Cut out a blossom, thread on to a short hooked piece of scientific wire and squash. When dry, tape 4–6 together. Add a very small ball of paste under the flower and add a calyx as for the flower. Colour as the flower. Make buds by moulding a small ball of paste on to a hooked 33 gauge wire. Press the point of a cocktail stick all over the top to give a texture. Dry. Add a calyx cut from two very small 5-pointed stars.

Assemble groups of flowers, buds and leaf cushions.

SEA HOLLY

flower

leaves

3-piece leaf

SEA CAMPION

flower

bud leaf

leaves

SEA BINDWEED

flower

leaves

calyx

THRIFT OR SEA PINK

flower

calyx

leaves

Rock Pool Scene

KEY TO THE DIAGRAM:

1 *oval raffia table mat*
2 *rocks*
3 *rock pool*
4 *grass*
5 *sea holly with 4 flowers and leaf groups with 4 large base leaves*
6 *sea campion with 3 flowers, 2 opening flowers, 2 buds and 8 leaf groups*
7 *sea bindweed with 3 flowers, 1 opening flower, 2 buds, and 6 small, 6 medium and 6 large leaves*
8 *thrift with 5 flowers and 9 leaf rosettes*
9 *starfish*
10 *mussels*
11 *sea lettuce*
12 *barnacles*
13 *crab*

Composition

The oval base is wired to a cakeboard covered with rolled fondant (sugarpaste). The rocks, made of rolled fondant (sugarpaste), are painted a pinkish orange colour. The taller rocks are positioned at the rear, creating a hole for the pool.

The flower groups are arranged between the rocks so they appear to grow out of the crevices. The sea holly is at the back with the sea bindweed creeping over the rocks on the right-hand side. The sea campion overhangs the pool and the thrift is positioned in front of them.

Royal icing grass is piped in white and painted when dry. The pool creatures are moulded with flower paste: the starfish is cut with a rose calyx cutter; the sea lettuce is cut with a carnation cutter; the mussels are moulded from egg-shaped pieces, cut lengthwise and painted black; the barnacles are made from flattened cones stuck to the rocks; the crab is moulded from flower paste. They are then coloured and steamed and, when dry, positioned in the empty pool. The pool is made by stirring some clear alcohol into greenish tinted piping jelly. This is then warmed gently until it becomes liquid and then poured into the pool a layer at a time so that it cools quickly and does not melt the sugar. Finally, semolina sand is sprinkled on the grass.

91

Autumn Hedgerow Flowers

As summer wanes, hedgerows abound with late flowers and ripening fruit and seeds such as deep pink wild fuchsia, violet-blue Michaelmas daisies, white bryony and dense clumps of bell heather.

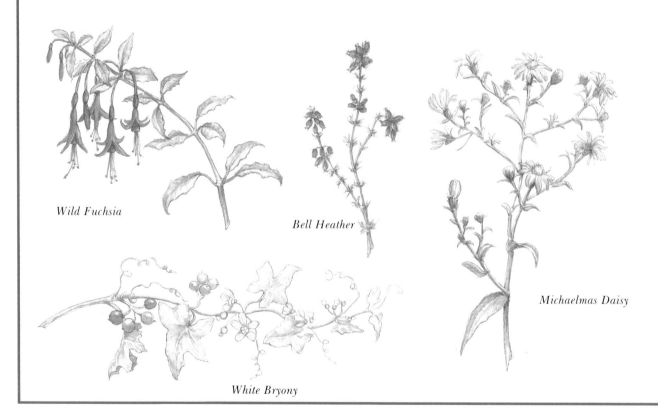

Wild Fuchsia

Bell Heather

White Bryony

Michaelmas Daisy

Anniversary Cake

Ideal for a late summer anniversary or wedding, the cake is displayed on a special artists' easel. The centre of the cake is cut out to form a frame and then covered with marzipan and cream rolled fondant (sugarpaste). The frame is made from rolled fondant mixed with gum tragacanth, and cut from a template. Ribbons decorate the cake and cakeboard. Leaves are made from rolled fondant.

Satin 'fabric', made from equal quantities of flower paste and rolled fondant, is arranged in the recess and attached with royal icing. The frame and fabric are dusted with silver snowflake and primrose sparkle for a satin effect. The spray is constructed in the hand, bound with wire, positioned in a plastic stem container placed in the cake and secured with royal icing. The hanging flower stems are finally bent into position.

THE FLOWER SPRAYS

- *5 sprays of fuchsia with 9 flowers, 28 buds, 8 opening buds, 5 stem leaves, and 15 very small, 15 small, 15 medium and 12 large leaves*
- *7 sprays of Michaelmas daisies with 14 flowers, 9 opening buds, 7 buds, and 7 small, 7 medium and 7 large leaves*
- *4 sprays of white bryony with 5 flowers, 8 opening buds, 12 buds, 20 berries, and 4 very small, 4 small, 4 medium and 4 large leaves*
- *4 sprays of bell heather*

Wild Fuchsia

Fuchsia magellanica

The tiny wild fuchsia grows in profusion in temperate areas. The corolla is deep purple with a long thin overcoat of deep fuchsia-pink. Groups of three leaves, buds and flowers hang all the way down the delicate stem.

REQUIREMENTS

● *White flower paste;* ● *medium seedhead and tiny pink stamens;* ● *white cotton thread;* ● *26, 28 and 33 gauge white wire;* ● *white tape;* ● *small ball tool;* ● *small rose-petal cutter;* ● *miniature dowel rolling pin;* ● *small fuchsia cutter;* ● *small centre tool;* ● *small scissors;* ● *modelling knife;* ● *wire strippers;* ● *glue;* ● *paste colours in red, blue and rose;* ● *cornflour (cornstarch);* ● *dusting colours in fuchsia-pink, red, cornflower-blue, black, white, moss- and apple-green.*

1 STAMENS: Group 6–7 tiny stamen heads together (not evenly). Place a single medium seedhead stamen (style) 1 cm (³⁄₈″) above the others. Bind with thread to a 26 gauge wire 5 mm (¼″) below the stamens. Trim and tape with ⅓-width tape. Dust the stamens with fuchsia-pink/red, then add a little water to the mix and paint the heads to deepen them.

2 COROLLA CENTRE PETALS: Cut out 4 small petals from purple flower paste (red/rose/blue paste colours). Thin the edges and cup with a small ball tool. Glue the right-hand third and place the second one over this. Add the other 2 in the same way to form a fan. Moisten the base of the fan, curve the stamens a little and place so that the threads are above the petals. Fold the left-hand petal over the wire, paint the edge and wrap the right-hand petal over it. With some cornflour on the fingers, squeeze at the base to secure to the wire. Dry reversed.

 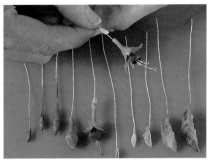

Make leaves in four sizes using the insertion method (see Basic Techniques, page 11). Insert the wire and crease down the central vein. Pinch the point and curve backwards. For the top stem leaves, cut an oval leaf from flat paste and sandwich a tiny hook on a half 28 gauge wire. For the top leaves, cut out tiny oval leaves (3 per stem) and fit to 33 gauge wire.

COLOURING: Dust the sepals of the flowers and buds and the upper part of the stem with red/fuchsia. Dust the ovary with moss/cornflour and over-dust the upper stems with the same mix. Dust the whole leaf with moss/cornflour. Add apple and cornflower-blue to the moss/cornflour and over-dust the upper surface. Vein with a sable brush and clean water. Edge dust all pieces with black and random dust with white. Steam and dry.

3 SEPALS: Make using the pedestal method (see Basic Techniques, page 11) from a large pea-sized ball of paste. Cut out with a fuchsia cutter. Make a hole in the centre with a small centre tool and thin and stretch the petals with a small ball tool. Cut a small triangle away between the petals with small scissors and thin these edges too.

Dust the inside of the flower with fuchsia/red dust. Pull the wire through so that the corolla fits into the hole. Thin below the flower by rolling between the first fingers. Trim to 5 mm (¼″) and round the base. Arrange the petals close to the corolla or curled backwards.

4 OVARY, BUDS AND LEAVES: For the ovary, thread a tiny ball of paste to the base of the flower. Mould it to a bullet shape. Curve the stem near the flower. For an opening bud, make the sepals as for the flower but mount them on a small ball of paste moulded to a hooked 26 gauge wire. For a bud, mould a small piece of paste into a 'candle'. Push a 28 gauge wire into the fat end. About halfway down, roll between the first fingers to form an hourglass shape. Indent a small ovary with the back of a knife. Make in various sizes – the tiny ones on 33 gauge wire.

5 ASSEMBLY: Take the top stem leaves and add 3 small leaves 1 cm (⅜″) below; tape together. Add 3 larger leaves and buds 2 cm (¾″) below. Add another larger group with opening bud and flowers on longer stems. As the flowers and leaves become larger they hang down more. Make several stems varying the flower and bud stages. Dust the stems with moss/cornflour and over-dust with red/fuchsia.

Michaelmas Daisy
A s t e r   n o v i - b e l g i i

Covered with small blue-violet daisy-like flowers, the Michaelmas daisy is a great favourite of butterflies.

REQUIREMENTS
● *White flower paste;* ● *medium yellow ball stamens;* ● *24 and 28 gauge wire;* ● *white cotton thread;* ● *tape;* ● *semolina;* ● *small and medium straight-sided daisy cutters;* ● *cornflour (cornstarch);* ● *modelling knife;* ● *small dog bone tool;* ● *egg white;* ● *dusting colours in lemon-yellow, violet, cornflower-blue, apple-green, brown, black, white.*

1 **FLOWER CENTRE:** Mould a small ball of paste to a hooked 24 gauge wire. Dip in egg white and then in semolina mixed with a little lemon dust. Dry.

STAMENS: Arrange 6–8 stamens around the flower centre and slightly higher and tie with thread. Trim and tape.

FLOWER: Cut out a small daisy from thin white paste and divide each petal into 3. Stretch and curl the petals with a small dog bone tool.

2 **FLOWER ASSEMBLY:** Thread and attach the flower below the centre. Make a second daisy with the larger cutter and attach in the same way. Pinch at the base to make the petals uneven and a bit untidy. Make smaller flowers using just the small cutter. Dry upside down.

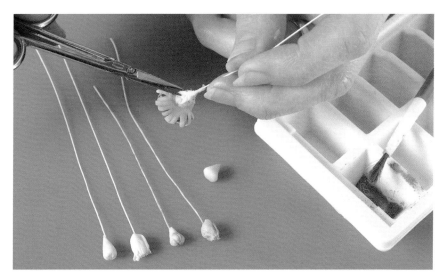

3 **COLOURING THE FLOWER:** Dust with cornflower-blue/violet/cornflour, avoiding the yellow centre.

BUDS: For an opening bud, mould a small ball of paste to a hooked 28 gauge wire. Make a small flower and mould around the ball. Dust as for the flower. For a bud, mould a pear shape on a hooked 28 gauge wire. Score 8 petal shapes with a knife. Dust just the top of the bud with the flower colour and the rest with apple/cornflour.

CALYX AND OVARY: Mould a small pear-shaped ball of paste, thread on to the wire and fix below the flower. With a small pair of scissors, make little wedge cuts all over with the points towards the flower.

4 **STEM LEAVES:** Slightly curve the stems of the flowers and buds. Attach 3–4 leaves down the stems below the calyx and alternating. Use the 2–3 tiny leaves for the opening flowers and buds.

LEAVES: Make using the insertion method (see Basic Techniques, page 11). Dry curving backwards.

5 **FINAL COLOURING AND ASSEMBLY:** Dust the calyx and stem leaves with apple/cornflour and a little of the flower colour and brown. Over-dust with cornflower-blue added to the mix. Dust the leaf with the same colour as the calyx. Add cornflower-blue and over-dust the upper side only. Paint the central vein with clean water to reveal the under colour. Edge dust all pieces with black and random dust with white. Steam and dry.

Take an opening flower and an opening bud and tape together with a small wired leaf at the junction using ⅓-width tape. Add a bud with a medium leaf 1 cm (⅜″) below this. Allow a similar gap and add a flower and large leaf. Make several sprays varying the position of the buds and flowers. These can be used separately or taped together with a large leaf at the junction. Dust the stems the colour of the calyx.

White Bryony

B r y o n i a   c r e t i c a

The white bryony is a vigorous tendrilled climber found in hedgerows, scrub and woodland. A near relation of the marrow and melon, it produces its berries in the same way from behind the female flowers. These are five-petalled and greenish white with darker veins.

REQUIREMENTS

● *White flower paste;* ● *porcupine quill or plastic cocktail stick (toothpick);* ● *sponge;* ● *maple or geranium veiner;* ● *small ball tool;* ● *5-point star cutter;* ● *miniature dowel rolling pin;* ● *28 and 33 gauge white wire;* ● *tape;* ● *fine lemon stamens;* ● *white cotton thread;* ● *modelling knife;* ● *cornflour (cornstarch);* ● *semolina;* ● *egg white;* ● *gum arabic solution;* ● *dusting colours in moss-green, apple-green, brown, orange, red, white, lemon-yellow, black.*

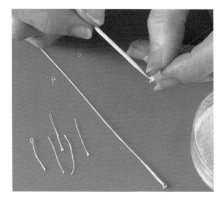

1 **STAMENS:** Take one strand of stamens and fold in half so that the heads are level. Paint the cotton with egg white so they stick together and dry. Make 5 groups for each flower. Tie the 5 groups together on a 28 gauge wire and cover with tape. Dip the heads in egg white and then in semolina mixed with moss dust. Separate the pairs with a cocktail stick. Dry.

2 **FLOWERS:** Roll paste very thinly and cut out the flower. Thin the edges with a small ball tool. Hollow and stretch the centre of each petal (*) and mark a groove down the centres. Place on a sponge to cup. Thread on to the wire bringing the petals to just under the stamens. Dry upside down. For a fully open flower work to (*) then reverse the flower on to a sponge and cup. Place on the wire as above.

Make tendrils by winding 33 gauge wire around the end of a paintbrush handle. Dust light yellow-green.

3 **CALXY:** Cut a very small 5-pointed star, cup and fix below the flower with the points between the petals.

BUDS: To make an opening bud, form a tiny ball of paste on to a hooked 33 gauge wire and dry. Cut out a flower, hollow the petals, cup, fit to the wire and mould around the central ball so that the latter is hidden. Add a calyx. To make a bud, mould a small piece of paste on to a 33 gauge wire and taper a little to the wire. Mark petals on the top with the back of a modelling knife. Mark a groove around the base with a cocktail stick. Make in several sizes.

BERRY: Form a ball on to a hooked 33 gauge wire. Push in a cotton from a large stamen and cut away so that just a small piece of cotton protrudes. Make baby berries from tiny balls of paste and thread below each flower and bud.

LEAVES: Make using the insertion method (see Basic Techniques, page 11). Crease the central and main lateral veins to roll back. Insert a 28 gauge wire.

4 **COLOURING:** Dust the flower with moss/white to produce a pale green flower. Dust the calyx, berry and stem with moss/cornflour. Add a touch of lemon to the flower centre. Add water to moss-green dust and paint fine lines down each petal and little dots between; repeat on the reverse side. Add more green in the centre.

Dust the buds pale green at the top and a medium green at the base and on the stem. Dust small berries light green, and medium ones green/yellow/orange; and large ones red. Paint the end cottons black. After steaming, dry and coat the red/orange berries with gum arabic solution to glaze.

Colour both sides of the leaves with medium-moss/yellow/cornflour. Over-dust the top side only with apple/moss mixed with a little yellow. Over-dust with the same green with brown added. Paint out the veins with clean water. Dust the stems light green.

5 **ASSEMBLY:** Tape together 3 buds, a small leaf and tendril. Add another group of flowers and buds 2 cm (³⁄₄") below the first. Finally add a group of berries with a large leaf.

Bell Heather

Erica cinerea

The bell heather is a brighter pink than the more spiky common heather and has fine whorls of dark green leaves.

REQUIREMENTS

● *White flower paste;* ● *white stamens with stiff cottons;* ● *cocktail stick (toothpick);* ● *26 gauge wire;* ● *white tape;* ● *modelling knife;* ● *white and dark green cotton thread;* ● *glue;* ● *white vegetable fat;* ● *cornflour (cornstarch);* ● *dusting colours in fuchsia-pink, violet, apple-green, brown, black, white.*

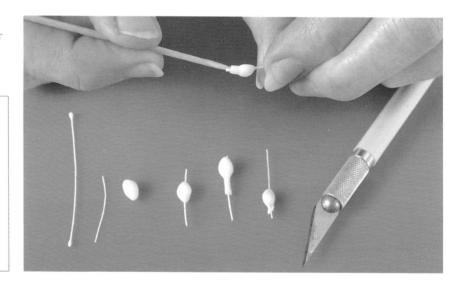

1 STAMEN AND FLORETS: Take one strand, cut in half and remove the heads. Apply glue to the centre of the half stamen cotton. Mould a small egg-shaped ball of paste and thread it up the cotton to the centre. Roll it at one end between the first fingers to tighten and to create a bottleneck shape. Trim this away so that just a tiny collar remains and push along to the end of the cotton so only the tip of the cotton protrudes from the collar. Use the end of a cocktail stick to open out the collar a little, and to indent so the floret looks like a tied oval balloon. Pinch 3–4 times to form ridges. Make in various sizes.

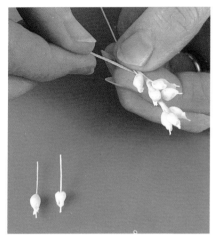

2 **ASSEMBLING THE FLOWER:** Tape a small floret to a half 26 gauge wire. Tape in 2 more a little below, and add another 2. Leave a small gap and tape in 2–3 more with another 2–3 below. Continue in this way making various length flowers with 7–15 florets per stem.

3 **COLOURING:** Dust the flower with fuchsia-pink mixed with a little violet/cornflour. Dust all the florets and over-dust with violet. Paint the stems and stamens with brown/cornflour with water added. Paint on the calyx, applying 5 small brush strokes from the base of each floret with apple-green/brown mixed with water. Over-dust the base of the florets with a very little black and random dust with white.

4 **LEAF WHORLS:** Whorls of tiny leaves grow at intervals down each stem. To make these, tie double knots of dark leaf-green thread – 2 to 4 to each group. This is a time-consuming job but the effect is very realistic.

5 **ASSEMBLY:** Make up some leaf stems and place them around groups of heather flowers.

WILD FUCHSIA

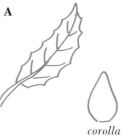

corolla

petal

leaves

MICHAELMAS DAISY

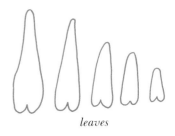

large flower   *small flower*   *leaves*

WHITE BRYONY

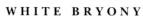

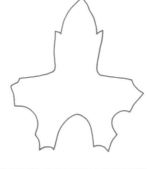

flower   *calyx*   *leaves*

BELL HEATHER

Autumn Hedgerow Scene

KEY TO THE DIAGRAM:

1 *rubberwood breadboard*
2 *stile*
3 *hedge*
4 *bank*
5 *grass*
6 *stones*
7 *wild fuchsia with 4 flowers, 5 opening flowers, 16 buds, 3 stem leaves, and 9 very small, 9 small, 9 medium and 6 large leaves*
8 *Michaelmas daisy in two groups: 4 flowers, 5 opening buds, 8 buds, and 4 small, 5 medium and 4 large leaves*
9 *white bryony with 2 flowers, 5 opening buds, 5 buds, and 4 small and 3 medium leaves*
10 *bell heather: 9 clusters of 4 to 7 bells each*
11 *tree stump*
12 *squirrel*
13 *magpie*
14 *hedgehog*
15 *soil*
16 *puddles*
17 *dead leaves*
18 *toadstools*

Composition

Rolled fondant (sugarpaste) banks are modelled in beige. The stile is cut from pastillage and grained with a cocktail stick (toothpick). Square holes are cut in the posts and steps to insert the horizontal bars and legs. When dry it is painted with beige/green liquid colour. The hedge is also modelled with pastillage to form a 'layered' hedge. Small branches are piped royal icing and the leaves are both piped with a small star and cut from flower paste with small cutters. The berries are simple piped dots. The stones and tree trunks are made from pastillage, as are the various animals. The wings and tail feathers of the magpie are made from flower paste.

Three stems of fuchsia are arranged by the hedge on the left with a group of Michaelmas daisies slightly in front of it by the path. A second small group is placed on the right. White bryony creeps forward on the ground over stones, while a clump of heather grows on the right-hand bank. Piped grass secures the plants.

Toadstools, made from flower paste, sprout by the hedge, trunk and stones. The path is sprinkled with light-brown sugar. The puddles are painted on with piping jelly, and the dead leaves (with the larger ones at the front to give depth to the picture) cut from flower paste and coloured tan-brown, red and black.

Useful Suppliers and Addresses

BRITISH SUGARCRAFT GUILD Wellington House, Messeter Place, Eltham, London SE9 5DP. Tel: (081) 959 6943.

JANE SHARP Courses, demonstrations, cutters and equipment. 12 Burhams Road, Ketton, Nr. Stamford, Lincolnshire PE9 3SJ. Tel: (0780) 721140.

A PIECE OF CAKE Suppliers of all sugarcraft equipment. 18 Upper High Street, Thame, Oxfordshire OX9 3EX. Tel: (084421) 3428.

SUGARCRAFT SUPPLIES PME (HARROW) LTD Suppliers of decorating equipment. Brember Road, South Harrow, Middlesex HA2 8UN.

POLYCONES (BOLT BOXES) CO Suppliers of cake dummies. 17 Beach Green, Shoreham-by-Sea, West Sussex. Tel: (0903) 63829.

J F RENSHAW LTD Suppliers of icings. Lock Lane, Mitcham, Surrey CR4 2XG.

THE HOUSE OF SUGARCRAFT Suppliers of decorating equipment. Unit 10, Broxhead Industrial Estate, Lindford Road, Bordon, Hampshire GU35 0NY.

WOODNUTS LTD 97 Church Road, Hove, East Sussex BN3 2BA.

SQUIRES KITCHEN 3 Waverley Lane, Farnham, Surrey GU9 8BB.

THE OLD BAKERY Decorating equipment. Kingston St Mary, Taunton, Somerset.

G T CULPITT & SON LTD Culpitt House, Place Farm, Wheathamstead, Hertfordshire AL4 8SB. Tel: (058283) 4122.

HAMMILWORTH FLORAL PRODUCTS LTD Suppliers of stamens, wires and ribbons. 23 Lime Road, Dumbarton, Dumbartonshire, Scotland G82 2RP.

JENNY CAMPBELL TRADING/B R MATTHEWS & SON 12 Gypsy Hill, Upper Norwood, London SE19 1NN.

CEL CAKES Suppliers of modelling tools. Springfield House, Gate Helmsley, York, North Yorkshire YO4 1NF.

CYNTHIA VENN 3 Anker Lane, Stubbington, Fareham, Hampshire PO14 3HF.

KNIGHTSBRIDGE BUSINESS CENTRE (WILTON UK) Knightsbridge, Cheltenham, Gloucestershire GL51 9TA.

DEPARTMENT OF THE ENVIRONMENT (WILDLIFE DIVISION) Tollgate House, Houlton Street, Bristol, BS2 9DJ. Tel: (0272) 218811.

NATURE CONSERVANCY COUNCIL Northminster House, Peterborough, PE1 1VA. Tel: (0733) 40345.

NORTH AMERICA

ICES (INTERNATIONAL CAKE EXPLORATION SOCIETY) Membership enquiries: 3087–30th St. S.W., Ste.101, Grandville, MI 49418.

MAID OF SCANDINAVIA Equipment, supplies, courses, magazine *Mailbox News*. 3244 Raleigh Avenue, Minneapolis, MN 55416.

WILTON ENTERPRISES INC 2240 West 75th Street, Woodridge, Illinois 60517.

HOME CAKE ARTISTRY INC 1002 North Central, Suite 511, Richardson, Texas 75080.

LORRAINE'S INC 148 Broadway, Hanover, MA 02339.

CREATIVE TOOLS LTD 3 Tannery Court, Richmond Hill, Ontario, Canada L4C 7V5.

MCCALL'S SCHOOL OF CAKE DECORATING INC 3810 Bloor Street West, Islington, Ontario, Canada M9B 6C2.

AUSTRALIA

AUSTRALIAN NATIONAL CAKE DECORATORS' ASSOCIATION PO Box 321, Plympton, SA 5038.

CAKE DECORATING ASSOCIATION OF VICTORIA President, Shirley Vaas, 4 Northcote Road, Ocean Grove, Victoria 3226.

CAKE DECORATING GUILD OF NEW SOUTH WALES President, Fay Gardiner, 4 Horsley Cres, Melba, Act, 2615.

CAKE DECORATING ASSOCIATION OF TASMANIA Secretary, Jenny Davis, 29 Honolulu Street, Midway Point, Tasmania 7171.

CAKE DECORATORS' ASSOCIATION OF SOUTH AUSTRALIA Secretary, Lorraine Joliffe, Pindari, 12 Sussex Crescent, Morphet Vale, SA 5162.

FER LEWIS, CAKE ORNAMENT COMPANY 156 Alfred Street, Fortitude Valley, Brisbane 4006.

NEW ZEALAND

NEW ZEALAND CAKE DECORATORS' GUILD Secretary, Julie Tibble, 78 Kirk Street, Otaki, Wellington.

DECOR CAKES RSA Arcade, 435 Great South Road, Otahaha.

SOUTH AFRICA

SOUTH AFRICAN SUGARCRAFT GUILD National Office, 1 Tuzla Mews, 187 Smit Street, Fairlan 2195.

JEM CUTTERS PO Box 115, Kloof, 3 Nisbett Road, Pinetown 3600, South Africa.

Index

ACKNOWLEDGEMENTS

I would like to acknowledge the support of all my students from the St Albans and Rutland (Leicestershire) areas for all their help and encouragement, especially my 'regulars' in 'proving' the designs.

I wish especially to thank Tombi Peck for her friendship and inspiration, Denise Fryer for her flower paste recipe, which I have used since Tombi gave it to me, and Jenny Walker and Norma Laver of A Piece of Cake for obtaining everything I needed. I must also thank Malcolm Craig and his team at Sugarcraft Supplies PME for their help and advice, and David Culpitt and his staff. Elaine and Stewart MacGregor at Woodnuts and Nick Lodge, who

was a fellow member in the early days of Guild in Sussex, must be remembered and thanked for their encouragement. Since then I have been a member of three different branches of the British Sugarcraft Guild and wish to remember and thank the friends I made at Thames Valley, Verulamium (St Albans) and Rutland as well as the branches I have visited. Other friends who deserve a special mention are those enthusiastic supporters from St Albans, Rosemary Smith and Jackie Venskuna.

Finally I must thank Cortina Butler, Gary Chapman and Joanna Lorenz and their team for making it possible to create this book.